Let's Do Life

Get Empowered to Live and Enjoy Life

T0171729

DAVID CONELLIAS

authorHOUSE®

AuthorHouse™ UK
1663 Liberty Drive
Bloomington, IN 47403 USA
www.authorhouse.co.uk
Phone: 0800.197.4150

Scripture quotations marked AMP are from The Amplified Bible, Old Testament copyright ©
1965, 1987 by the Zondervan Corporation. The Amplified Bible, New Testament copyright
© 1954, 1958, 1987 by The Lockman Foundation. Used by permission. All rights reserved.

Scripture quotations marked KJV are from the Holy Bible, King James Version
(Authorized Version). First published in 1611. Quoted from the KJV Classic
Reference Bible, Copyright © 1983 by The Zondervan Corporation.

Scripture quotations marked NKJV are taken from the New King James Version.
Copyright © 1982 by Thomas Nelson, Inc. Used by permission. All rights reserved.

Published by AuthorHouse 02/16/2015

ISBN: 978-1-5049-3620-0 (sc)
ISBN: 978-1-5049-3621-7 (hc)
ISBN: 978-1-5049-3622-4 (e)

Print information available on the last page.

Any people depicted in stock imagery provided by Thinkstock are models,
and such images are being used for illustrative purposes only.
Certain stock imagery © Thinkstock.

This book is printed on acid-free paper.

DAVID CONELLIAS

Anything is possible to him that believes . . .

CONTENTS

ACKNOWLEDGEMENTS

First of all, I give thanks and honour to God, my heavenly beloved Father, for allowing me to write my first book! Father, it is because of Your imparted knowledge, wisdom, and understanding that all of this is made possible. Thank You for engrafting into my DNA all that You would have me be and for making me become all You have destined me to be. Thank You for making every resource that I needed available and for helping put everything together by Your Spirit. Above all, thank You for loving me unconditionally and for being patient with me. I am forever grateful, and I love You dearly with all my heart.
Your Loving Son, David.

To my dearest parents and mentors, Dr Walter Masocha (Dad), and Dr Judith Masocha (Mum): Thank you for your prayers, guidance, love, and support. All these years of grooming and teaching me were not in vain! It's because of your grooming that I am were I am today. Thank you for helping me discover who I really am and for pushing me towards destiny. I am forever grateful. *With much love, respect, honour and appreciation from my heart.*

To my beautiful beloved mothers, Mrs Mary Chikukwa (Mother) and Mrs Rosemary Chibwe (Momz): Thank you for your love, support, and "lectures" I am so blessed to have such wise and virtuous women in my life, and yes, I will rise up every morning and call you blessed, because you are! Thank you for being there, and most importantly, for believing in me. I hope I make you proud.

Mum (Mary), thank you for everything, and for such selfless love. You played a big part in this project, and I wouldn't have come this far without your help in so many ways. Thank you for pushing me to destiny, and for having my back.

Loads of love, respect, honour, and appreciation from my heart to both of you.

I would also like to sincerely thank my dear sister Monét and my brother-in-law Thuli, and the rest of my huge family and friends for their love and support. Thank you for encouraging me and pushing me to become the best that I can be. I dedicate this book to each and every one of you. And to everyone reading this book, thank you for your support and for believing in me and accepting this beautiful piece of work. I dedicate this book to each and every one of you as well. Sandra, Sharon, Joy, Tinashe and Tafadzwa, the crazy bunch, thank you for everything guys, and for being the craziest and loving brothers and sisters. When is the next holiday?

I love, appreciate and cherish you all guys!

And finally, my dearest brother Munashe Chibwe. Thank you for re-educating me on my basketball and chemistry; those lessons are priceless! Your input on *Principle #20* is of great value and importance. You did an astounding job, and I hope I was a good student throughout the process! Thank you for taking part in history making; believe it or not, you actually inspired the whole section on the principle of joy and laughter. How ironic is it that you were even busy sending me jokes when I was typing up this portion of the book? Remember "Mr Miyagi"? Hahahaha, exactly!! I'm dedicating the whole of *Principle #9* especially to you. Not a day goes by without you sending me a joke, or doing something funny to make me laugh. I sincerely thank God for you, from the bottom of my heart. Keep the laughter roaring! *With much love, appreciation, respect and honour*

Your dearest brother, David.

FOREWORD

Here is yet another confirmation that we serve the Almighty God, the God of Abraham, Isaac, and Jacob, in a new vision for a new generation, experiencing the unconditional (agape) love of God. Indeed it's God's love for all: Agape for all nations!

A young man writes an inspirational book that is sure to benefit both the old and the young.

Those who have written books have put structure to it in the traditional form of "chapters". David, in true "new generation" style, comes up with a new approach – he uses "principles" instead of chapters. Principles build character, and character begets integrity. No doubt the principles in this book, if applied consistently, can lead one to a healthy, vibrant life. People of all age groups, races, and colours can benefit from this book.

Apply the principles and learn to live life to the full. Yeah, *let's do life*!

Dr Walter Masocha

INTRODUCTION

Everything starts with an idea, which when acted upon develops and becomes reality. The same is true about this book. This book serves to inform and simply empower both the young and the old, religious and non-religious, scholar and non-scholar, all people of all nations from various walks of life. I am not here to preach a message to you, but to share with you some simple and yet fundamental principles I have come to learn in life.

Now let me warn you: the content in this book is *very* dynamic. I touch on topics that affect everyday life, from health to finances, spiritual things and non-spiritual things. It only requires the reader to keep an open mind and enjoy the ride. I'm certainly no life coach according to the standards of this world, but I'm someone who definitely breaks the rules, thinks outside the box and is overly observant. I believe that empowering people is one of my many gifts, whether I have the qualifications or not. This is something that education cannot teach me to do but something that's innate. I was born with it, and I'm definitely not afraid to make use of it!

In this book, I decided to use my creative side and call the chapters *principles*. So be warned: if you are looking for the word *chapter*, you won't find it; it's a new thing!

Why be principled? Principles are what set you apart as an authentic person; they help define the type of person, or individual, you are. Principles are simply a set of rules, or code of conduct one adheres to, thus forming a foundation for a system of beliefs or chain of reasoning. I believe having the right set of ethics and principles as an individual contributes significantly to your success and quality of life. I set a challenge for you to go and draft a list of your own set of principles you would like to adhere to on a daily basis. Follow your own rules and be consistent in application. Along with being principled, add integrity and character to it.

The Purpose-Driven Life According to Daniel

A life lived on purpose is a life worth living. Purposing in your heart not to merely survive but to live is the difference that sets you apart from the one who merely lives and is driven by any wind that passes by. It was because of being purposed that Daniel was set apart from all of the other Jews who were held captive in Babylon, including his very own friends. The Bible says Daniel purposed in his heart that he would not defile himself with the portion of the king's delicacies or with the wine that was served at the king's table (Daniel 1:8). Daniel took a bold stance, would not back down from what he believed in, and would not break God's law (given in the Pentateuch), because he was a principled young man, full of integrity. The Pentateuch was a set of instructions (law) given by God, which the Jews had to adhere to, and so Daniel purposed in his heart to please God and follow His commands rather than fear mere man. Even when faced with false accusation, because he would not bow down and worship any other god (King Darius) beside the one true God of Abraham, Isaac, and Jacob, Daniel chose to rather be thrown into the den of lions and die at the mercy of God than disobey and displease God Almighty. It was this bold stance of faith in God that caused God to send an angel and shut the lions' mouths so that they could not touch God's beloved (Daniel 6). Daniel had purposed in his heart to only serve the one and true God, and therefore his purpose would drive his actions, attitude, and behaviour – it controlled him. It is not surprising that the Bible says he was found to be of an excellent spirit! Principles-driven by purpose, and integrity, breed excellence.

While his friends are mostly remembered by their Babylonian names (Shadrach, Meshach, and Abed-Nego, instead of Hananiah, Mishael, and Azariah), only Daniel is remembered by his original name, for he would not accept to be called by a strange name; he knew who he was! Daniel found favour in the sight of God and men, and the Bible says he and his three friends were ten times better than all the wise men in King Nebuchadnezzar's realm! Kings would inquire from Daniel because God gave him wisdom and understanding of dreams. He was highly regarded in Babylon, and yet he was a Jew, a foreigner in that country where Jews were held captive. Daniel would outlive at least three kings, and in all their reign, all three kings acknowledged Daniel and set him above the princes of the nation! Daniel did not change who he was, or bend to his surroundings or environment, but he maintained his integrity to the end! He was never choked up by peer pressure. He dared to be peculiar and unnatural in the sight of the world, and yet so natural and perfect in God's sight. How many of us drop our values for the sake of pleasing others or change because of surroundings or company? Think about that!

When your heart is inclined to a certain purpose, principles are what will set you on the path to achieving your goals. Choose to be like Daniel. He would not bend to the rulers of this world or dance to their tune. He only danced to the tune of the Most High God. Live a purpose-driven life. Purpose in your heart to forgive, and you will. Purpose in your heart to serve and revere God wholeheartedly, and let your fruits be evidence. Purpose in your heart to love, and you will. Purpose in your heart to be a peacemaker, and you will. Purpose in your heart to succeed, and surely you will. Purpose in your heart to always be on time, and you will. Purpose in your heart to think and speak positively, and you will enjoy the fruits thereof. Purpose applies in anything and everything; it's all about making the right choices. Let the right purpose and set of mind be the driving force that propels you to living life in abundance, influencing your every decision and choices. Live a purpose-driven life guided by principles and maintain your integrity.

Like my father always says, no one can claim monopoly over knowledge. Everybody has got different formulas that work for them in life, and the only difference is that I'm putting mine to pen. Be encouraged and empowered as you read this book, and above all, implement whatever catches your attention (preferably everything). Don't rush as you go through the principles; take your time and write down some notes like good students who want to learn and better themselves. Come on, *let's do life* together, and let's get empowered to live and enjoy life.

Principle #1:

SEEK YE FIRST; PRAY

In the beginning, God
—Dr Walter Masocha

Prayer Changes Everything
*Prayer is the master key, it unlocks and opens doors
that need to be open and unlocked, and it shuts and
locks the doors that need to be shut and locked.*
—David Conellias

Growing up in a little town called Kirkcaldy, I remember developing a routine were I would wake up at 4 a.m. in the morning just to pray and seek the face of the Lord. It was during these early hours of the morning I had the most wonderful experiences in His presence. I understood the value and benefit of starting my day with God, and not involving Him as an afterthought. Putting God first is a principle I've learnt from my father and mentor, and I quote his catch phrase that says, "It always pays at the end to involve God in the beginning". Put God first, and you will never be last. Prayer is simply communication between man and God, and I believe it also involves implementation of His Word. Just like any other relationship, communication is vital in order for that union to be sustained. The more you communicate with God, the deeper in love you fall with Him and the more you increase the depth of intimacy between yourself and God. Prayer should be a dialogue, where we talk to God and He in turn speaks back to us. Learn to take time to listen in your heart and spirit what God is saying. This is when leaving a Spirit-led life comes into play. God is always speaking, and it only takes us to listen intently and follow His lead through His Spirit inside us. In our conversation with God, that's when we take the time to make known our requests and petitions to Him, with the faith and knowledge that He is able to do exceedingly and more abundantly than what we can either think or imagine. God cannot do anything for us until we learn to ask Him to intervene on our behalf in prayer. He gave us dominion over the earth (according to Genesis), and what happens here on earth is in our hands. Whether He intervenes on our behalf or not is completely up to us. Also, whether we choose to obey His Word or not is completely up to us as well, because He gives us the freedom to choose, and we have to use it wisely. It is only through obedience to His word, that our prayer life is effective and enhanced! Because that word is life, and is like a map that directs us to the answers we search for.

Psalm 115:16

New King James Version (NKJV)

The heaven, even the heavens, are the LORD's;
But the earth He has given to the children of men.

Many times we get caught up in the business of life that we forget the most important principle of involving God in the beginning. Take time to pray every day before you start your day and before you carry out a particular task. The Bible says in Psalm 37:23 *"the footsteps of a righteous person are ordered of God"*. When you involve God in the beginning, when you give Him the permission to intervene or interject, you allow Him to order your steps and guide you in what direction you should go. Many of us can save ourselves the trouble if only we learnt to apply this principle at the beginning of the day, or before a task, even before we make decisions. In the beginning God first!

Proverbs 3:5-6

New King James Version (KJV)

Trust in The Lord with all your heart and lean not on
your own understanding, in all thy ways acknowledge
Him, and He will direct your paths.

Prayer is indeed the master key, and prayer changes everything. When you involve God in the beginning through prayer, you give heaven the permission to invade the earth realm on your behalf. Prayer has no geographical limitation, because your words carry weight and are either the solution or barrier to someone's need. When we pray, we demonstrate our trust in God and not in our own abilities. Every time I pray and commune with God, I come out of my closet feeling empowered. I always have this sense of overcoming, and I'm ready to tackle whatever comes my way. That's what prayer does; it empowers you, it rejuvenates you, it revives you, and you feel refreshed, especially if its quality time spent with God. Prayer makes you come out with a different and positive perspective on life. You begin to see things in a positive light. Every time you spend time with God, He pampers you with His anointing (for we are His bride). It's the unction of the Holy Ghost that gives you the "supernatural ability" to conquer the unconquerable. You'll be able to pull things out from the spirit realm into the natural, and operate in a dimension where you don't negotiate for breakthroughs. I want you to always remember that when you affirm big, believe big, and pray big, big things happen! Keep that thought in mind. Consistency is vital to sustain this power of prayer. Everybody wants power; we are all fighting to be in control of our circumstances and situations. That's the longing for power, because one who is not in control has no power to change circumstances! And that power can be gained when we learn to earnestly seek the face of God in prayer and fasting! Prayers that are enforced with fasting are very destructive to the enemy. The enemy is not afraid when you read the Word (because he knows the Word as well); he is more intimidated when you read the Word, put it into action and reinforce it with prayer and fasting. If the enemy can keep you away from praying, he would have succeeded, because he knows the power therein. Don't give him the satisfaction.

Don't just depend on other people's prayers (dependency syndrome); learn to fast and pray for yourself, because God wants relationship with you, and not just your grandmother. Pray for yourself, pray for family members, pray for your children, and pray over your businesses. Speak what you want to see achieved in your businesses through prayer. Prayer does not have to be complicated. The most important thing is that you believe in your heart what you are praying for and about. You can pray in your heart whilst on the bus to school or work. You can pray whilst taking a walk in the park (a power walk is what I call it) You can pray anywhere and at any time. If we are to pray without ceasing like Jesus said, then prayer has to be incorporated into our busy lives each and every day. Also make sure you have a dedicated time for prayer where you are not doing anything but just humbling yourself before God and focusing on Him. Get into that prayer closet and draw strength from it.

Our Father

God in His office as king has got many titles. We know Him as God, Lord, King, Master, Saviour, and Ruler. Furthermore other attributes are associated with His name (our Provider, our Healer, our Peace, our Redeemer, our Righteous Judge, our Husband, etc.). When Jesus taught us to pray (Matthew 6:9–13), He taught us to approach God as *God, Our Father.* Look at the characteristics of a good earthly father. He provides for his family and never abandons his children. A good father takes time to listen to his children when they are speaking (and even if doesn't make sense sometimes, a father will understand the message because he knows his children). Good fathers are patient, loving, caring, and nurturing, and they bless their children. What I've noticed about children is that the word *busy* does not exist in their vocabulary; they are not afraid to approach their dads, even when their dads seem busy. They depend so much on their fathers for anything and can disturb their fathers at any time. To them their dads are like superheroes who are invincible (too powerful to be defeated) and can tackle anything. This is why I believe Jesus said, "If we are not like little children, we will not enjoy the benefits of the Kingdom of Heaven" (Matthew 18:1–6).

When we approach God, we must be humble and trusting like the little children. God is not a God who is after you to destroy you: He is not a fault-finding God, looking for an opportunity to pounce on you. But He is a caring and loving Father, who just wants to be there for us if we let Him and only if we approach Him with boldness and confidence in His fatherly nature. Yes, a good father chastises his children to drive foolishness out of them, but it's all out of love. If you never disciplined your own children, they would go wild and bring dishonour to you and the family. God corrects us as the loving Father He is, just like we discipline our own children when they misbehave. David even says, "Better is the correction of God, than that of man." God is not there to harm or to kill you, but His corrections build you up and mould good character. He is the potter, and we are like clay in His hands. And when it comes to answering our prayers (petitions, requests), Jesus even says, "Whatever you ask for in my name, this I will do, that the Father may be glorified in the son" (John 14:13). God is a god who blesses His children so that their joy is fulfilled and they have abundance of all things. When I grasped this concept of literally approaching God as a father, I started calling Him *Dad* even in my prayers. That's how personal I get with God. Why not do the same when you approach His throne. He's got nothing but love for you. He is Abba Father! Pray to your Father who is in heaven (not on earth) and who seats upon the throne as the King of Kings and the Lord of Lords!

Power in Prayer

Be a house of prayer because you are the temple of the Lord. Talk with the Holy Spirit just like you do with the next person. The Holy Spirit is not "a thing" but a person, a being, and you can talk to Him as a friend. He is the friend who will never turn you away but who is there to listen as you empty out your heart to Him. When your heart is overwhelmed, He is willing to calm your fears and will lead you to the rock that is higher (Psalms 61:1–2). When you are set on the rock that is higher, it means you gain advantage over anything that has troubled you. "Come unto me all that labour, all that are troubled and tormented, cast your cares on me for I care for you," (Matthew 11:28-29). Go to Him, and let Him apply salve to the wounds the enemy has inflicted upon you. When you are healed, you are able to function effectively and also heal others in turn.

Apart from healing, prayer gives you spiritual insight. It is through prayer that you can have access to the spiritual realm and command things to happen on your behalf by the power of God. Depending on the types of prayers you make, angels are dispatched on assignment for your words' sake. Look at Daniel and how he prayed and fasted for twenty-one days without ceasing until an angel came with his answer. The angel was sent on assignment the very first moment Daniel opened his mouth to pray, but Daniel's answer was blocked by the prince of Persia (read Ephesians 6:10–18). There was war in the heavenlies, and for Daniel's sake the archangel Michael had to intervene so that Daniel could get his answer. Soon Daniel's answer came because he was consistent in prayer; he prayed without ceasing. Sometimes the enemy will try and usurp answers to your prayers. The Bible clearly states that God is not deaf and that His arm is not too short to save (Isaiah 59:1). The moment you set your heart to pray, God hears. When the enemy tries to block your answer, constant prayer is like fire burning his hands until he finally releases what's rightfully yours because of the power and pressure of your words. Don't give up and don't be discouraged when you see nothing happening. As a matter of fact, as long as you believe God for what you are praying for and never doubt, something is already in motion. Let your prayers continue to be steadfast and hot (fervent); let them be cause for war on your behalf in the spiritual realm. Many of us have aborted our answers, because we gave up too quickly instead of continuously praying like Daniel. This is why Jesus encourages us to pray without ceasing. We have to keep pushing through heaven's door until a breakthrough comes our way. (Read Daniel 10)

It was only through prayer that Daniel received the prophecy of the Messiah (Daniel 9). He prayed again when put in the lion's den, and the lions could not touch him (Daniel 6). Esther fasted and prayed when the Jews faced annihilation, and she helped save her people by standing in the gap for them before the King. The way Esther stood in the gap to plead for her people before the King is a perfect example of successful intercession for others (Esther 8). The Jews' enemy Haman the plotter died instead of the people he persecuted. When Elijah prayed, the heavens withheld rain for three years, and there was drought in the land. When he prayed again, it rained, and the land was restored once again (1 Kings 17, 18). The church prayed for Peter when he was bound in prison chains, and by the power of prayer, Peter got released from prison supernaturally (Acts 12). Elisha prayed and raised a dead child back to life (2 Kings 4). In the Psalms and the books of Kings (even Chronicles and Samuel), we read of David's victories against his enemies, which took place because he was a prayerful man. David prayed and defeated Goliath when Saul's army became afraid of this gigantic enemy. David did not see the magnitude of the giant but an opportunity to demonstrate God's power and show that God *is* the Almighty! Instead of magnifying the problem, David acknowledged the magnificence of the Almighty. It is only through prayer that we get such boldness (1 Samuel 17, eps. v. 45–47). Check the words David spoke inverse 45 - 47(The Power of Confession. What you boldly utter in prayer is paramount to your breakthrough). It is of great importance to note that David did not waste time praying the problem, but he prayed the answer he wanted to see. His bold declaration commanded the armies of the Living God to act! Follow through the story and see what happened to Goliath and the dramatic way he fell after God intervened.

1 Samuel 17:45–47
King James Version (KJV)

Then said David to the Philistine, Thou comest to me with a sword, and with a spear, and with a shield: but I come to thee in the name of the LORD *of hosts, the God of the armies of Israel, whom thou hast defied. This day will the* LORD *deliver thee into mine hand; and I will smite thee, and take thine head from thee; and I will give the carcases of the host of the Philistines this day unto the fowls of the air, and to the wild beasts of the earth; that all the earth may know that there is a God in Israel.*

And all this assembly shall know that the LORD saveth not with sword and spear: for the battle is the LORD's, and he will give you into our hands.

It was this bold stance and declaration, demonstrating David's faith in the Living God, that caused God to move and act! Hannah, who was barren, prayed for a child and gave birth to a prophet (Samuel), who would give counsel and advice to kings (1 Samuel 1:10–20). Jacob prayed, and Esau's mind was changed after twenty years of seeking vengeance (Genesis 32, 33). Jehoshaphat prayed, and God confounded the hearts of his enemies; they were turned away.

The Bible is full of instances where people prayed and God answered. Prayer requires a clean heart. It's important that your heart is right before God, so that nothing hinders your prayers. The Bible says, "If I harbour iniquity in my heart, the Lord will not hear me" (Psalms 66:18). Confess your sins before the Lord first, sincerely ask for forgiveness, and forgive others in turn. Let Him cleanse you with the blood of Christ, and let the water that Christ shed at Calvary wash your sins away, as He clothes you with Christ's righteousness, so that when you appear before Him, all He sees are the works of His Son Jesus completed in us. The Lord is gracious and abounding in mercy. He will hear you and forgive you. Just believe it in your heart. Pray with an understanding of the times, and pray speaking the prophecy given over your life just like Daniel did.

Mitigating the Works of Darkness

Prayers released by faith and through fasting, are like missiles and take on the form of spiritual atomic bombs, causing nuclear type explosions in the realms of the heavens. Blast your way into victory over the attacks of the enemy. Ascend into the realm of power. The higher you go in God, the more dangerous you become to the enemy.
—Cindy Trimm

Ephesians 6:10–18

King James Version (KJV)

Finally, my brethren, be strong in the Lord,
and in the power of his might.
Put on the whole armour of God, that ye may be
able to stand against the wiles of the devil.
For we wrestle not against flesh and blood, but against
principalities, against powers, against the rulers of the darkness
of this world, against spiritual wickedness in high places.
Wherefore take unto you the whole armour of God, that ye may be
able to withstand in the evil day, and having done all, to stand.
Stand therefore, having your loins girt about with truth,
and having on the breastplate of righteousness;
And your feet shod with the preparation of the gospel of peace;
Above all, taking the shield of faith, wherewith ye shall
be able to quench all the fiery darts of the wicked.
And take the helmet of salvation, and the sword
of the Spirit, which is the word of God:
Praying always with all prayer and supplication in the Spirit, and
watching thereunto with all perseverance and supplication for all saints.

It is through fervent effectual prayer and fasting and through the help of the angels that we can effectively weaken the forces of darkness by the power of God. The words we declare and utter cause angels to respond on our behalf, executing the commands we give in prayer. Ephesians 6:10–18 is clear when it says that our battle is not against flesh and blood but against principalities, powers, rulers of darkness, and spiritual wickedness in high places. These are all different levels in the kingdom of darkness. When the enemy attacks you, he sends a spirit that instigates the attack. For every evil work, there's a spirit behind. That's why we need to show no mercy and take no prisoners when it comes to praying against such enemies. The problem is not the person being used as point of contact, the problem is the spirit behind the action, counteract every spirit with the Word of God. Pray against the spirit and not against the person. If you are praying and speaking ill and destruction against the person (flesh and blood), how different is it from witchcraft? Spiritual warfare may come in form of opposition, trials and tribulations, false accusations, character assassination, feelings of rejection, battling of negative thought cycles, illnesses and disease, and anything that causes you to lose your peace. Know how to deal with every spirit on every level.

The enemy also uses people that are close to you, so that when the attack comes, it deeply hurts, aggravates and paralyses you if you let it. He uses the people that you might hold dear. He doesn't go very far; there's a Peninnah in everyone's life (1 Samuel 1: 1–28). It can be your own family, children, church members, or co-workers. Even Jesus was betrayed by one of his very own disciple, Judas. David the king was at war with his own son Absalom; Hannah's spirit was constantly grieved by Peninnah. Most of the times the enemy will keep using the same person over and over again to vex your spirit (like in Hannah's case). The enemy's intent is to try and distract you and cause you to be sorrowful, because once you are in that state, you become unproductive. That's why we ought to be aware of his every device and be on the lookout for such people used as the enemy's playground. Keep your eyes open! Be like Hannah instead. When her soul was grievously troubled, she earnestly and relentlessly sought the Lord, prayed until mistaken for being drunk, and eventually got her answer from God. Whilst she was pregnant with her first son, heaven was pregnant with a prophet to the nation of Israel. Amazing!

One thing you have to know about the enemy and his forces is that they are illegal here on earth because they do not possess a physical body. Therefore he is in constant search of a body he could use to initiate his evil works. He is a spirit being without a physical body. The earth was given to man, and God created a body for man to dwell here on earth as human beings with a spirit (soul). So without the physical body, a spirit does not belong to the physical realm, but to the spiritual world, and cannot operate legally in the physical unless there's a body to use. The same principle applies with God. When He wants to execute His plans, He looks for an available body to use for His glory. That's' why He then pours His anointing (divine supernatural unction) and Holy Spirit on man, so that man is able to do what He couldn't do in the natural. You see, God even obeys His own rules and principles.

The enemy is a copycat. He tries to imitate what God does. The only difference is that his works are evil, of darkness, and meant to destroy and oppose God's purpose and plans on earth and in us. However, when we fervently fast and pray (displaying passionate intensity, vehement, ardent, sincere, heartfelt, emotional, spirited, zealous, whole-hearted, and earnest), being in right standing with the King (righteousness), our prayers avail much (James 5:16). Righteousness is key and is simply aligning yourself with God's Word and putting your faith in Him without wavering! Both your feet have to be firmly fixed in the Lord and not partially.

Put on the whole armour of God, so that you might be able to resist the enemy and stand your ground when the day of evil comes, Paul says. The armour makes you resilient. When pressure is coming in from all angles of life, as long as you have the armour, you will not break under the weight of trials and tribulations! The armour consists of:

- Truth (the truth sets us free through the Word of God).
- Breast place of righteousness (when your breastplate is intact, protecting your chest cavity where your heart is, the enemy's weaponry and devices will not be able to infiltrate your soul).
- The gospel of peace covering your feet (a child of God is a peacemaker, wherever you go you must live peace in the hearts of the people and not aggravation).
- The shield of faith which will quench the fiery darts of the enemy (how big is your faith? Faith has the power to undo what the enemy meant for harm. Faith is like water that puts out fire caused by the enemy, activate this power.)

- And finally the helmet of salvation and the sword of the Spirit, which is the Word of God.

How effective are your defences against the enemy when he attacks? Put that armour on for your own protection against his whiles, and release the atomic power of prayer! Not only is our stance against the enemy on the defensive side, but we ought to also take up an offensive position. There's no time to relax. "Watch and pray," Jesus said *(Matthew 26:41)*. Our eyes ought to always be open, because we are not ignorant of the enemy's devices. We are well aware of them and quick to shoot his arrows down when he tries to attack!

As an aid, the Psalms are full of Scriptures we could use against the enemy. For example, read Psalms 140 and 144, and draft up your own prayers of offence against the enemy using God's Word.

Note: Be careful not to endorse negativity and the works of darkness by what you wear, watch, listen to, and read. Some of us have become ignorant in this area. These are some of the things that can lure evil spiritual forces into our lives when we drop our guard and entertain them. Don't open the door for the enemy. Whatever door you have opened, command it to be shut, and do away with everything that has got his fingerprints on it! Be careful, and be on the lookout.

Pray for Others

Don't just pray for yourself, but learn to pray for others, because the answer that you might be looking for will come when you learn to be selfless in prayer. Pray for someone else's success; sacrifice some time to fervently pray for someone else's breakthrough as if you were praying for your own needs to be met. When you do this, I guarantee you, God will see your need as well and act on your behalf. This is a principle that has definitely worked for me. If you are someone driven by jealousy and struggle with this point, ask God to "thresh" jealousy out of you. Pray for someone else's ministry, family, or business, and let it not end there, but let your prayer be backed up with action. Go and bless someone, someone's ministry, someone's family, and so forth. If you have the financial means or resources to help someone, then I say do it! Don't ask God to do something for someone that you are well capable of doing! God has blessed you to become a blessing. So learn to bless others, and your prayer life is fulfilled.

Pray about everything and anything. Trust me it pays in end. When in doubt, pray; when afraid, pray; when sad, pray; even when you are happy or joyful, pray at all times. *You can never pray enough.*

Pray for the Nations
Praying men are the vice-regents of God; they
do His work, and carry out His plans.
—E. M. Bonds

Be like Daniel, Esther, and Nehemiah, and stand in the gap for your nation and for your people. You might be the breakthrough they are looking for if only you would arise and pray. Pray for governments, nations, cities, and even the country where you live. Pray for peace in your own nation and even other nations, because it will be to your advantage. Pray for those in authority. Pray for the way they govern the country; pray that any laws they pass, will not negatively impact you or the people around you. Pray for economic and financial tides to turn in your nation's favour. Pray for an increment in your nation's GDP and GNP. Pray that every evil work in your neighbourhood is mitigated. Pray for healing of civil unrest, illegal countermands, pandemic disease, racial harassment, and prejudice of any sort. Pray for the atmosphere within your nation to be filled with the glory of God and for the will of God to prevail. Pray for systems, institutions, cultures, environments, regulations, policies, codes, legislation, and ordinances to be influenced by the Holy Spirit. You are the one who holds the key to your nation's prosperity. If only everybody would understand this principle and unite in effectively praying for nations. Be like Daniel, who prayed fervently for his nation. Earnestly pray for God's will to prevail in your nation, and be the catalyst that aids in the dominance of God's plans in your neighbourhood or nation. It is our number one priority and mission as children of God to see God's kingdom and God's will reinstated in our neighbourhoods and within the hearts of the people around us.

Jeremiah 29:7
New King James Version (NKJV)

And seek the peace of the city where I have caused you to be carried away captive, and pray to the LORD for it; for in its peace you will have peace.

Seeking First His Kingdom
When we pray God's word, we get God's results.
—Yolanda Adams

When you involve God in the beginning, you demonstrate how much trust you put in Him. Just like children trust their father for protection and guidance when crossing a busy road, we should demonstrate that same kind of trust towards God. When going through the highway of life, you need the Father's hand to hold on to and guide you, because the Father knows better. The Bible also says, when we seek God first, His kingdom, and His righteousness (His dominion, His way of doing things, His commands, His statutes, His way of thinking; because *His thoughts and ways are higher than ours*), all the necessary things we so desire to have in life, and even on a daily basis are added to us without even asking for them. Why? Because we dared let Him take the lead by involving Him in the beginning and by following His principles first, and His ways of doing things! Put God in the front, and implement His statutes and commands, and the rest of life and every good thing it has to offer will follow you in abundance.

Thy Kingdom Come, Thy Will Be Done

God is *the King*, and He is the King of Kings and the Lord of Lords. Those who accept Him through Jesus Christ become a part of His domain as children of the kingdom of light. A king is never voted into power or voted out of power! God is the ancient of days who has been before everything else was. No matter how much some may deny Him and His power, they could never abolish the fact and truth that He exists and that He is sovereign. His stature is unchangeable! How interesting is the fact that we are part of His domain and under His dominion; but He has also given us our own domain (earth), so that we represent His nature (glory) here on earth and reinstate His kingdom here on earth. Wow! When we please the King by doing what He commands, the King has no option but to shower us with blessing, because of our faithfulness and loyalty to Him and to His dominion. And in turn the spiritual domain (through its King) impacts our physical domain (the earth and personal surroundings). Seek first to please God, and He will put everything that pertains to your life in order. Thy kingdom come, and thy will be done! *Let your kingdom, Father, impact the kingdom you have entrusted me with as your vice regent!*

Just like any other government or kingdom, the kingdom of heaven has fully established departments to cater for the needs of God's children. Learn to tap into God's endless supply of resources by accessing these departments through prayer. If you need healing, call on *Jehovah Rapha* (Exodus 15:26; department of health); if in need of provision, call on *Jehovah Jireh* (Genesis 22:14, department of welfare); if you need peace, call on *Jehovah Shalom* (Judges 6:24, department of peace). All of these and many others are functional departments in the kingdom. Take note of all the other names of God and use them to your advantage. As Jesus taught us, pray, "Thy Kingdom Come, and Thy will be done on earth as it is in heaven" (Matthew 6:9–13). As citizens of the kingdom of heaven, it is the King's will for us to have all these benefits found in the kingdom. Hence, why we need to claim them through prayer. It is the King's duty and pleasure to look after His citizens for His reputation's sake. The good thing about God is He's not only concerned about His reputation, but He loves us dearly and would have us prosper. When you invite His kingdom to impact your kingdom, you give His dominion and rule precedence over your own, and in turn you reap the bountiful benefits found in His kingdom. Everything that was misaligned has to come back into order because the light has come.

These are some of the things that complete or fulfil our prayer life. Prayer should be a lifestyle that involves communication with God, implementation of His Word, worship, and the right actions and attitude towards others. Peter encourages us to be alert and sober-minded, so that we may pray. The state of your mind matters when you approach God in prayer, a sober mind breeds positive thoughts (1 Peter 4:7). Watch and pray indeed without ceasing; keep knocking on heaven's door until the King responds! Bother Him all you want because eventually He will come through. Pray for the will of the King to prevail in your life and the lives of others around you. Pray for Him to reveal what His will for your own life is. Pray for God's will to prevail over your nation and other nations. Let the will of the King of Heaven prevail over our lives and realm. Learn to inquire from God concerning His will and purpose over your life, the lives of people around you, and over your nation. When you spend quality time with God in prayer, your ears become pressed against His heart, and your heart picks up the heartbeat of the Father. It beats synchronised and syncopated to the movements of the Spirit. You become concerned about the will of the Father, and your desire is to see His will fulfilled here on earth.

The subject on prayer is quite vast and broad, and this is just a summary. I've only scratched the surface so that at least we have a basic foundation on prayer and fasting. The rest is up to you. Study the Scriptures, and receive divine revelation by the Spirit of God.

Purpose to live a prayer-driven life!

Principle #2:

READ THE MANUAL

Thy word is a lamp unto my feet, and light to my path.
—King David

The Word of God is infallible. It is truth, alive, undisputed, and sharper than a double-edged sword. It penetrates even to the dividing of soul and spirit, joints and marrow; it judges the thoughts and attitudes of the heart! The Word of God is *the* manual to life, and those who accept and apply the principles therein reap the beautiful rewards. Joshua says it all:

Joshua 1:8
New King James Version (NKJV)

This book of Law shall not depart from your mouth, but you shall meditate in it day and night, that you may observe to do according to all that is written in it. For then you will make your way prosperous, and then you will have good success.

Everybody wants success, but success is not success unless it's *good* success. Why are some prosperous but still sorrowful? They lack the basic fundamentals, which can only be extracted from the Word of God. I don't want to have billions of pounds accessible to me and still be miserable. From what I understand, the blessing of the Lord makes rich, and no sorrow is added to it. If success comes with sorrow, it's not good success, because it's not blessed. Read the Word of God for good success. His Word is light, life, and very much alive. When we have the Word of God inside, it is like the compass to life itself. From it, we get guidance and direction. It contains the solutions to all of life's problems because it is the manufacturer's handbook. God created us, and as the manufacturer of life, He gave us the manual to life, which is His Word. If you want to know how to operate and be in control of your own life, read the manual, extract the principles within the manual, and adhere to them.

David poses the question in Psalm 119:9: "How can a young man keep His ways pure?" He answers it by saying, "By taking heed according to Your word". He even adds, "Your word have I hidden in my heart, that I might not sin against You". Sinning against God, or breaking His code of conduct, only creates a gap between us and God (see principle #20). When this code of conduct is broken and there is no repentance, there are always consequences. To repent is to simply reconsider your ways and get back in line with the King's precepts, which is His Word. His Word is used for reproof and correction. It helps us stay on the right course of life.

The Word of God is good news. It delivers and sets us free (Psalm 119:70); it brings hope and comfort (Psalm 119:49–50). By it, our faith is strengthened because faith comes by hearing and hearing by the Word of God. When that word is spoken over us, that light illuminates our path and makes us view life from a different perspective full of hope and assurance (Romans 10:17). The entrance of His Word gives light and understanding to the simple, and your heart or depth of understanding are enlarged. It gives light and direction (Psalm 119:32,105,130); it is proven (Psalm 18:30); it is like an unquenchable fire (Jeremiah 20:9; 23:28–29), it is God's wisdom (Jeremiah 8:9). The Word of God brings great peace, when you are full of it. Nothing offends you and nothing moves you or causes you to stumble (Psalm 119:165). The Word of God is an offensive nuclear weapon in the armour of a Christian, which should be fired up by the power of prayer. A Christian who is not armed by prayer and the Word is bound to fall when trouble comes. Without this sword of the Spirit, which is the Word of God, your defenses against the enemy of life are inadequate (Ephesians 6:17). His Word is sweeter than honey (Psalm 119:103), and it is liberating (Psalm 119:45). Liberation comes to those who are bound by the prison chains of religion or any other chain that might hinder freedom of worship and relationship with God. True freedom comes when we pursue to live by the fruit of the Spirit (love, joy, peace, longsuffering, gentleness, goodness, faith, meekness, and temperance; Galatians 5:22–23). Galatians 5 states that against such there is no law; the law becomes void when there is no fruit of the Spirit as the foundation. Therefore in order for the law to be fulfilled, the fruit of the Spirit has to be the foundation of the law; and where the Spirit is in control, there is liberty (2 Corinthians 3:17). Observing the Word of God brings favour with the King (Psalm 119:58), and it brings life to the afflicted (Psalm 119:50, 93). From His Word we extract wisdom and knowledge by reading the book of proverbs. Our worship lifestyle is enhanced by reading the Psalms. The Psalms not only help us in our worship time alone with God but also encourage and inspire us. The Word of God also lets us see Christ's lifestyle here on earth (in the synoptic gospels), so that we can emulate and follow His perfect example and teachings about life on earth and in the kingdom of heaven. The Word of God is simply rich and full of power to the one who believes in its dynamic content.

We are to meditate on it *day and night* if we are to make our ways prosperous and have good success. To meditate is to ponder upon His Word, to deliberate, to reflect, and to think deeply about its contents. Meditation can also be a sweet murmuring; to murmur is to speak softly, talk softly, whisper, mutter, or mumble. Here confession of the Word comes into play when we produce that sweet murmuring from our lips. It is a way of planting the incorruptible seed into your heart. When you confess the Word through your sweet repetitive murmuring, you are writing it upon the tablet of your heart so that it sticks on you for good. In order for mediation to be complete, implementation has to come into play as well, and then your meditation is fruitful. Whether you confess it softly or aloud, it's still meditation. Always bear in mind that God is a servant of His Word. According to Jeremiah 1, God watches over His Word to perform it, and according to Isaiah 55:11, His Word never returns to Him void (never ever). It always accomplishes that which He has sent it forth to accomplish and prospers in that which He has sent it to prosper. Now in this knowledge, be encouraged! His Word is the perfect key to success, because every principle I'm going to talk about in this book is found in the Word of God. The world might not acknowledge it, but some of the rules and regulations that govern some of the prosperous governments of this world are extracted from the Word.

True Wealth

Wealthy nations like the United Kingdom and the United States are prosperous and successful today because of their ancestors who used the principles in this Great Book. They sought after and worshipped God. Even on the American dollar bill you find the inscription "In God we trust." We are enjoying the benefits of our wise ancestors today because they left us this wealth which they attained by observing the commands of God. They obtained favour from God in all their dealings, and wisdom through His Word. God the King blessed them with wealth which could be passed on to generations. Even the Bible says, "A good man leaves an inheritance for his children, and his children's children," and this is exactly what our ancestors did. By following the principles found in this manual, they made their ways prosperous and attained wealth, which could be passed on to many generations long after they are gone. They paved the way for us, and now we bask in the benefits. It's sad that the modern generations are drifting further away from God and his Word. They desire to make up their own manual to fit what they think is right in their eyes. They have made up their own god, who can shift and bend to what they want. What a shame! God's Word is the greatest source of our ancestors' great wealth. Now that some drift away from God Himself, what inheritance will they leave for the next generations to come if their moral and ethical conduct is not guided by God's Word?

This does not only apply to nations but to individual families as well. The greatest gift you can give to your children is the Word of God. The

Word will keep them right. As long as the children are trained up in the way they should go, when they grow up, they will not depart from the teachings contained in the Word (Proverbs 22:6). When you give them the treasure of the word, it's their duty to keep passing this treasure on to generations that come after them. The secret is in the method of *training* that determines the outcome of your children when they come of age. With what methods are you training your child? What treasure, what inheritance are you passing on to them? It is only through the Word that true wealth is obtained. When you have the Word, you have everything that pertains to life. You have the secret to abundance, joy, peace, and love.

It's the Solution

Whatever situation or crisis you might face in life, there's always a solution in this Great Manual. You find the answer to health problems, financial and economic problems, marital problems, family problems, and any other problem we might think of. The Word deals with our fears, anxieties, depression, stress, insecurities and anything that inhibits life in abundance. When your life truly epitomises the Word of God, you operate successfully in all the dimensions of life (faith, prosperity, health, power, wisdom, knowledge, and understanding). The Word of God is wealth at its best!

It Is Law

The Word of God is also like a piece of legislation, a decree passed by the King of Kings, to be obeyed and never to be negotiated (hence the terms *precepts, statutes, testament, testimony* and *book of law*). It is the law of God. It is the will of the King, partitioned into two (Old Testament and New Testament) for us to enjoy as its beneficiaries. Just like any piece of legislation, you need a lawyer to help you decode the contents of the book. Now the lawyer in this instance is the Holy Spirit. He is the one who, as Jesus said in John 14:26, "will teach us all things" and cause us to understand what the natural mind cannot comprehend in its own capacity, because He is "our Helper," and "Teacher". The Helper and Teacher is the one who helps us decipher this code of law; He understands it because He is the Lawyer. He is the one who will make us aware of what inheritance the King has given to us His beneficiaries. If you try to reason with things of the Spirit with a natural mind, it will only boggle you; hence the need of the Lawyer's services for us to understand. Before you read the Word, ask the Lawyer to help you understand this beautiful and liberating manual. Ask Him to open your eyes, that you may behold the wondrous things contained within His law (Psalms 119:18).

Challenge: *Your challenge is to come up with a daily Bible reading plan, to help you get as much as you can from this manual. Meditate on it, pick a Scripture, ponder on it, and murmur it softly throughout the day, so that it sticks to your heart. It is my prayer that my life epitomises God's Word!*

Read Psalm 119 in its entirety.
Purpose in your heart to live a life guided by the Word of God!

Principle #3:

LIVE LIFE IN ABUNDANCE

Life should be vibrant and dynamic, accept
change, and make some changes too.
—David Conellias

John 10:10
Amplified Bible (AMP)

The thief comes only in order to steal and kill and destroy.
I came that they may have and enjoy life, and have it
in abundance (to the full, till it overflows).

Ask yourself, Am I enjoying life? Do I have life in abundance? Many of us are not enjoying life and are definitely not living life in abundance. We are more of worriers and stressors than life livers! We worry about bills, relationships, jobs, and so forth. Whatever worries you, whatever stresses you, whatever makes you lose your peace of mind is a thief! The thief not only refers to the devil, but anything that makes you lose your sleep or causes unrest is an enemy and a thief, because it has stolen what God desired for you to have, and that is life in abundance. Don't get me wrong. Yes, we face challenges here and there, but the key point is to stay focused on God and not to lose sight of Him, because the moment we lose sight of Him unrest, fear, and every negative thought cloud and choke us up.

Make up your mind today: I will not lose my peace or let anything or anyone steal my joy. I shall not be moved; worry and anxiety shall not be my portion!

Having life in abundance does not mean not having challenges or problems but having peace and calm in the midst of a raging storm. It means being able to smile when there's nothing pretty to smile about, it means having peace and joy when there's chaos all around you. (I like what one wise man once said: "There is value in chaos.") When you live life in abundance, you are stress free, worry free, and always at peace by choice. (You have to make up your own mind not to be bothered by every little or big thing that comes as a distraction.) Having life in abundance means still being able to peacefully rest and sleep even when your children are acting crazy, your husband is out of control, and you don't know where your next meal is coming from (depend on God to provide). Having life in abundance has got nothing to do with having plenty of money but with having plenty of God in you. When you have God, you have all the wealth you could ever dream of. God desires that we prosper, for He is our Shepherd and makes us lie down in green pastures. He leads us beside the quiet waters and restores our souls. He refreshes us and pampers us as long as He is inside and a permanent fixture of our lives. Focusing on problems only creates even more problems, but focusing on possibilities may lead to breakthroughs. You attract what you spend your attention on.

Do Not Worry

Jesus commanded us not to worry for a reason. We are commanded not to have anxiety about anything but in everything to make our requests known unto God in prayer. I'll give you some scientifically proven facts about worrying and stress. Then you'll understand why we are commanded not to worry. Worry takes away from the life we are supposed to have and enjoy! So stop worrying in abundance and start living life in abundance.

Matthew 6:25–34

Amplified Bible (AMP)

*Therefore I tell you, stop being [a]perpetually uneasy (anxious
and worried) about your life, what you shall eat or what you shall drink;
or about your body, what you shall put on. Is not life greater [in quality]
than food, and the body [far above and more excellent] than clothing?
Look at the birds of the air; they neither sow nor reap nor
gather into barns, and yet your heavenly Father keeps feeding
them. Are you not worth much more than they?
And who of you by worrying and being anxious can add one unit
of measure (cubit) to his stature or to the [b]span of his life?
And why should you be anxious about clothes? Consider the lilies of the
field and [c]learn thoroughly how they grow; they neither toil nor spin.
Yet I tell you, even Solomon in all his [d]magnificence (excellence,
dignity, and grace) was not arrayed like one of these.
But if God so clothes the grass of the field, which today is
alive and green and tomorrow is tossed into the furnace, will
He not much more surely clothe you, O you of little faith?
Therefore do not worry and be anxious, saying, what are
we going to have to eat? Or, what are we going to have
to drink? Or, what are we going to have to wear?
For the Gentiles (heathen) wish for and crave and diligently seek all these
things, and your heavenly Father knows well that you need them all.
But seek (aim at and strive after) first of all His kingdom and
His righteousness (His way of doing and being right), and then
all these things taken together will be given you besides.
So do not worry or be anxious about tomorrow, for tomorrow will have
worries and anxieties of its own. Sufficient for each day is its own trouble.*

Chronic Stress, the Mother of Anxiety and Worry

Stop worrying and over stressing, it makes you age quicker!
—David Conellias

According to research, stress is a normal physical response to events that make you feel threatened or upset your balance in some way. When you perceive danger, whether imagined or real, your body's natural defences kick into high gear in a rapid, automatic process known as the "fight-or-flight-or-freeze" reaction or stress response. This is a way the body protects you. When working properly, it can help you stay focused, energetic, and alert. In emergency situations, stress can save your life, giving you that extra strength to defend yourself, for example, slamming your brakes to avoid an accident. It is what helps you rise to meet challenges, or drives you to study for exams when you would rather be watching TV.

But beyond a certain point, stress stops being helpful and starts causing major damage to your health, mood, productivity, relationships, and quality of life. It is important to realise this risk when your stress levels are out of control. Stress affects the mind, body and behaviour in many ways and can lead to serious mental and physical health problems.

Symptoms of stress:

- ❖ Memory problems
- ❖ Lack of concentration
- ❖ Negative outlook
- ❖ Anxious or racing thoughts
- ❖ Poor judgement
- ❖ Constant worrying
- ❖ Moodiness
- ❖ Short temper
- ❖ Inability to relax (you are agitated)
- ❖ Sense of loneliness and isolation
- ❖ Depression (you have no joy)
- ❖ Aches and pains
- ❖ Diarrhoea and constipation
- ❖ Nausea
- ❖ Chest pain, rapid heartbeat

❖ Eating more or less
❖ Sleeping too much or too little
❖ Procrastinating or neglecting responsibilities
❖ Nervous habits

Effects of chronic stress:

The body doesn't distinguish between physical and psychological threats. When stressed over a busy schedule, an argument with a friend, a traffic jam, or a mountain of bills, your body reacts just as strongly as if you were facing a life-or-death situation. Long-term exposure to stress can lead to serious health problems such as

❖ Pain of any kind
❖ Heart disease
❖ Depression
❖ Weight problems
❖ Digestive problems
❖ Autoimmune diseases
❖ Sleep problems
❖ Skin conditions, such as eczema
❖ Hair loss

I can relate to the skin conditions, because once I became so stressed over a particular issue that I was not able to eat or sleep properly. I would lie awake every night wondering what was going to transpire when everything was ruled out. I began to develop spots on my skin similar to the ones you get when you have chicken pox, but it wasn't chicken pox. When I prayed over the issue, that's when the Lord revealed to me that my condition was caused by stress. Yes, chronic stress can eventually physically affect your body. so stop overstressing. Instead of stressing, why not be positive and be optimistic? Your positive thoughts and words will help calm the situation. When stressed, try and focus your mind on positive thoughts, walk your dog, go to the gym, or pray and read the Word of God. Find ways that can bring a positive distraction and help you cope better. Avoid being alone when under immense stress. Surround yourself with positive people.

Positivity vs. Negativity

Stop worrying and start living. Live life with a passion, be passionate about life. When you wake up, take a deep breath and thank God for giving you another chance to live, because not everyone made it to face another day. Let your heart be full of praise and thanksgiving. Again I reiterate what we already know and say; stop worrying and overstressing. Worrying doesn't add value to the life you are supposed to have and enjoy! A little positive thought in the morning can set the mood for the day, and the same is true with a negative thought. Refuse a spirit of negativity; it alters your perception towards life. A negative spirit causes your world to appear grey and grim, removing the colourful dynamics of life. Negativity affects your mood, and you might also hurt the people around you. Negativity definitely has an effect on your health; it affects your immune system. Negativity breeds apathy (lack of interest, enthusiasm, or concern). When you have a spirit of apathy within you, you abort purpose and undermine your own potential. You feel you have nothing to live for. You become unresponsive, unsupportive, slothful, stubborn, indifferent, visionless, and depressed. Everything about you becomes dull.

Spice It Up and Don't Get Bored

A little change and spice here and there can go a long way. People often get bored in life, and sometimes the reason is doing the same thing over and over again. You follow the same routine day in and day out, and you always get the same results. There should be no one set routine to your everyday life, but you should learn to try out different things and spice it up a little bit. Instead of having one route to work every day, why not try and find if there's a different one that you could use for change? Don't get stuck in one cycle of doing things; change can prove beneficial and avoids monotony. One main important key I've come to learn about life is moderation. Too much of something is not good! Don't expect to get different results either when you keep doing the same thing over and over again. If you want different results from what you've been getting, change the way you've been doing things.

> *Insanity is doing the same thing over and over*
> *again and expecting different results.*
> —Albert Einstein

Take time to go out and meet different people. Personally, I love travelling. I like to go to different countries and meet different people with a different lifestyle and culture to mine. I find it quite refreshing when I go to different parts of the world. It adds colour to my life. It puts the excitement in life and makes me look forward to something different every year. Have a hobby that you thoroughly enjoy. It might be music, going to the opera, or attending concerts. It might be playing basketball with family or friends, painting, reading, swimming, or photography. Don't be afraid to try out different things. Have a great sense of adventure and fun; go for horse riding lessons or for excursions. Whatever rocks your boat, go out and enjoy it. Colour your life. You are the artist, and the paint brush and colour palette are in your hands, produce a **piéce** de **résistance**; God gave you the freedom to do so. Life should be vibrant and dynamic. Accept change and make some changes, too. Invest into your own life; put something into it before you can get something out of it.

Socialising with friends and family is a good way of bonding with people you love, but do it with the right company. Because the company you spend time with will affect the quality of your life. Choose wisely whom you allow to take up your time. Not all unions are fruitful and mutually beneficial. I will discuss this point further later on in the book. Now let's take a look at the rest of the major principles, because they also affect the quality of your everyday life.

Note: Always re-invent yourself, it is the person who is most adaptable to change who survives the longest, no matter what the circumstance is, they always come out winning and are always at the top of their game.

Keep Moving Forward; Don't Look Back

If you are depressed, you are living in the past. If you are anxious, you are living in the future. If you are at peace, you are living in the present. Past is waste paper, present is newspaper, and future is a question paper! —Warren Buffet

The reason why your eyes are in front and not at the back of your head is because our focus should be ahead and not backward. God put your eyes in front of your face as a reminder that you need to have forward focus, because everything you need is ahead and in front of you. It is more important to look forward than to look backward. The funny thing is for some of us, our eyes are at back of our heads; we have backward vision, and we are living in the past instead of living in the present and looking forward to what's ahead of you. Your past can be a hindrance to progress if that's where your focus is, but those who keep looking forward, despite past circumstances, progress no matter what, because they are focused in the right direction. Looking back can be good for reflection purposes, and only if you are remembering for the right reasons. Other than that, stay focused ahead. Know where you are going, because if you don't know, you'll probably end up somewhere else. Keep your eyes fixed on your goals and don't look backward.

Isaiah 43:18–19

Amplified Bible (AMP)

Do not [earnestly] remember the former things; neither consider the things of old. Behold, I am doing a new thing! Now it springs forth; do you not perceive and know it and will you not give heed to it? I will even make a way in the wilderness and rivers in the desert.

Remember ye not the former things, neither consider the things of old. Even God instructs us not to dwell in the past or to consider things of old. What's in the past is now in the past. If you made mistakes before, learn from them and use them as a stepping stone to move forward. Don't let the bad things that happen in life define who you are; don't let them destroy you but let them strengthen you. Be resilient; use the storms of life to your advantage, just like an eagle uses the storm's wind to lift it high up above the clouds. Relish the challenges and use them profitably. God desires to do a new thing in our lives every day, every season. Shall you not perceive, comprehend, deduce, understand, see, sense, and know it? He poses a question. Have the eye that sees what God sees ahead for your future; have the eye of faith. Look at what He says next: "I will even make a way in the wilderness, and rivers in the desert." What used to be a barren land in the past can become a fruitful land in the future if we only learn to trust Him and have forward vision. Take Him at His word! Live in the present and just enjoy life. Stop worrying about what tomorrow holds or what could be. Don't give up on life because life has so much to offer if you steer your attitude in the right direction. The way you see your future is much more important than what might have transpired in the past. I like what Zig Ziglar says: "Getting knocked down in life is a given, but getting up and moving forward is a choice." When you have the eye of faith, you learn to take each day as it comes, step by step, brick by brick, mile by mile with hope and an optimistic outlook. Live in the moment. Don't allow tomorrow's worries clutter your present but seal them out of the container called today! Stop worrying about what could be; eliminate the negative and employ only positivity.

My Mission in life is not merely to survive, but to thrive; and to do so with some passion, some compassion, some humour, and some style. —Dr Maya Angelou

Purpose in your heart to live life in abundance and not to be choked up by the cares of this world!

Principle #4:

GUARD YOUR HEART, WATCH YOUR ATTITUDE

*Your heart is like a garden, be careful with what seeds
you allow to grow in that garden, because they will
germinate and produce after their own kind.*
—David Conellias

Purging the Soul

Guard your heart with all diligence, for out of it flow the issues of life.
—King Solomon

Your heart is the hub of the soul, and what you allow to enter and sit at heart affects your soul, which is the very essence of you. Your soul comprises of the mind (Logos), emotions, feelings, spiritedness (*thymos*), and Eros (appetite, desire). It is the aspect of your whole being that integrates, correlates, and brings to life everything about you. You are a living soul with a body. I was amazed to learn that scientists have proven that the soul has real substance and weight. In 1907, the researcher Duncan MacDougall conducted an experiment to prove the difference in weight between an animal and a human being after death. Because animals don't have a soul, there was no difference in weight; however the experiment on human beings showed that they all measured 21 grams less after death, proving that human souls have got weight and substance. We need to understand the significance of that number 21 when we look at biblical algebra: The number 21 is divisible by both 3 and 7. The numbers 3 and 1 signify divine completion (the trinity – 3 in 1; Father, Son and Holy Spirit operating as one God). The number 7 is referred to as the number of God; it represents divine perfection and spiritual completeness. The similarity and connection between these numbers is not by coincidence. Furthermore, if you add 2 and 1 together, you still come back to the number 3. This makes us understand God when He says we were created in His image, because all these numbers add up to His divine nature, which He impressed into man when He breathed the breath of life into us (Genesis 2:7), and we became living souls.

When your soul is contaminated, life itself is contaminated with that which clutters your soul. Therefore it is important to watch what you allow to enter and sit at heart! When your soul is out of sync with the Spirit, remember Psalm 103. Tell and command your soul to bless the Lord and all that is within you! Those who have the urge to commit suicide have got a spirit of abortion of purpose and the spirit of death tormenting them. Don't let the enemy of life cause you to give up your soul to him. Take good care of the very you, which is your soul. A heart full of God's Word nourishes the soul, causing it to function with sound judgement.

> *A man's mind may be likened to a garden, which may be intelligently cultivated or allowed to run wild; but whether cultivated or neglected, it must, and will bring forth. If no useful seeds are put into it, then an abundance of useless weed seeds will fall therein, and will continue to produce their kind.*
>
> —James Allen

I liken your heart to a garden, and you are the one to tend after that garden. Guard your garden (heart) with all diligence, for out of it springs forth issues pertaining to life. What seeds do you sow in the garden of your heart? Are they seeds of good or evil? Are they seeds of gossip, malice, and slander, or seeds that build up and heal others? Are they seeds of love or hatred? Are they seeds that bring forth life or seeds that lead to death? The thoughts you harbour in your heart are expressed through your attitude towards others and life in general. Your thoughts, determine your attitude; your attitude determines your actions and the words you speak; your actions and words eventually determine your destiny! What are you gravitating towards as you feed your soul through your heart?

Just as a gardener attends to his garden, keeping it free from weeds, and growing the flowers and fruits which he requires, so may a man tend the garden of his mind, weeding out all the wrong, useless, and impure thoughts, cultivating toward perfection the flowers and fruits of right, useful, and pure thoughts.
—James Allen

Do Not Let Your Heart Be Troubled

The Heart

Your heart can also refer to your deep inner thoughts – yes. But I want to talk about the natural human heart. I recently discovered that the human heart (the organ) is recognised by scientists as a highly complex system with its own functional *brain*, and we know that a brain is responsible for thoughts amongst other things as well. It makes sense that God would say, Do not let your *heart* be troubled. God meant it literally, because He knows what capabilities He has put in the heart. The heart pumps blood to the rest of your body, and we know that the life of an individual is contained within the blood and that the heart is the engine that regulates life throughout your body. Not only that; the heart is also a sensory organ and a sophisticated centre for receiving and processing information. The nervous system within the heart (heart brain), enables it to learn, remember, and make functional decisions independent of the brain's cerebral cortex. Furthermore, the signals that the heart continuously sends to the brain influence the function of higher brain centres involved in perception, cognition, and emotional processing.

What you process (think) in your heart has the power to influence your brain's thought cycle. I believe God created the heart to govern the brain, but once we stop thinking from our heart, the brain assumes control thus forming the logical thought process. Then when logic steps in, you have a problem, because if something doesn't make logical sense, it's impossible to achieve or execute. It is in your heart that faith and the power of belief are made alive. What seemed impossible becomes possible in your heart, and your heart can override the brain's logical way of thinking. Logic is good, but it can limit you. It is so amazing how the human heart is so powerful. It even starts beating in a foetus before the brain develops. When pregnant women go for a scan, the first thing the doctor or midwife checks for is the heartbeat. If a heartbeat is established, there is life. And another thing to note is that, even after the brain is dead, the heart can still function without the brain!! This shows how powerful God made the human heart! It is the engine of life, and everything to do with life stems from it. The heart is the centre of human life. When there is no heartbeat, you are dead.

The heart is obviously linked to the brain and the rest of the body. It communicates information to the "main brain" and throughout the body via electromagnetic field interactions. The heart generates the body's most powerful and most extensive rhythmic electromagnetic field. Compared to the electromagnetic field produced by the "main brain", the heart's field is apparently 60 times greater in amplitude, and it permeates *every* cell in the body. (Wow, God is simply amazing.) Having a magnetic component which is five thousand times stronger than the "main brain's" magnetic field, the heart can outwardly affect surroundings within a 10-metre radius. This explains why, when you walk into a room full of tension, you feel the tension. It's radiating from the electromagnetic field of people's hearts within the room. That's why my father always says, "Attitude is contagious, is yours worth catching?" It's all to do with the signals that are radiating from within your heart. The heart's ever-present rhythmic field has a powerful influence on processes throughout the day. The brain rhythms naturally synchronise to the heart's rhythmic activity, and during sustained feelings of love or appreciation, the blood pressure and respiratory rhythms, among other oscillatory systems, entrain to the heart's rhythm. Simply put, the energy that comes from the heart interacts with the rest of the organs in the body. They all follow the heart's rhythm. Our emotional state is communicated throughout the body via the heart's electromagnetic field, and the rhythmic patterns of the heart change significantly when we experience different emotions.

When your heart is troubled, everything to do with life and your overall well-being is in trouble. (This also explains why Jesus said Mark 11:23, "If you believe it in your 'heart' and do not doubt, then it shall be done according to your faith." Why? Because your heart has got the power to influence surroundings and everything about you.)

This subject is closely linked to the previous principle of living life in abundance. Do not let your heart be troubled. A troubled heart dries up your spirit and literally sucks the life out of your bones. When your heart is troubled, you have no peace or joy, are always in distress, and have no peace of mind. When your heart is troubled, you lose the very essence of life, which is living life in abundance. Learn to take control of your circumstances and not the other way round. Command your soul (intellect, mind, heart) to bless the Lord, tell your thoughts to align with God's Word, and have an amazing and optimistic attitude towards life.

As a Man Thinketh in His Heart, So Is He

Proverbs 23:7
Amplified Bible (AMP)
For as he thinks in his heart, so is he. As one who reckons, he says to you, eat and drink, yet his heart is not with you [but is grudging the cost].

Could it be that things are the way they are because of your thoughts? You are a sum total of your thoughts! This subject is very important, because everything starts in the mind. Your world is framed by your thoughts first, and the words you speak. What do you think of yourself?

Are your thoughts healthy? Do your thoughts build up your life or destroy it. You are exactly what you "think" you are, just like the Bible says. This is a biblical truth that affects our daily lives and quality of life!

If your thoughts are of evil, your lifestyle will follow suit and the fruits of your evil thoughts will surface. If your thoughts are pure and of good, the fruits will also show! Only pain and sorrow follow an evil heart, but joy and peace follow a heart full of pleasant thoughts! Your own body is a servant of your mind. It's amazing how our thoughts can even affect our bodies and health. Some of the diseases people carry are a direct result of unhealthy thought cycles, and you have the power to change that. Break the cycle and liberate your soul! The more pure and positive your thoughts are, the more your overall health and well-being improves. I dare you to try it and see the results!

If You Believe It, You Can Achieve It

If you can conceive something in your mind, you can achieve it as long as you believe it in your heart. It's all to do with mind over matter! What you tell your mind in your heart becomes reality. If you tell your mind you cannot achieve a thing, in reality it becomes true. You can't really take your feet where your mind has never been! The power of thought even affects the singer. Before they hit that high note, they have to be able to do it in their mind first. Otherwise, if their mind restricts them, the note will be impossible to reach. The mind will send signals to the body causing their body to tense up all the necessary muscles involved when singing, thus affecting overall performance. Whatever the mind can conceive and believe, the mind can achieve, regardless of how many times you have tried and failed in the past or how lofty your aims and hopes may be. Think of your mind as a padlock. It can either lock up possibilities or release them. The power to harness that effect solely lies within you. You are the one who controls the function of the padlock, because the keys are in your hands.

God gave everyone *the gift of the mind. Use that power to control your thoughts to whatever ends you desire.*

Some of us need a paradigm shift if we are ever going to experience progress or success in life. We need to break through the strongholds and barriers created in our minds, because sometimes the only obstacles we face were created by *us* by way of thinking. Once you change your thinking pattern, everything else aligns itself according to your change in attitude. Like I said before, attitude is simply a state of the mind. Others are misinformed and have been taught the wrong things from childhood. The wrong type of seeds might have been planted into our thoughts through what our parents or other people said over us, and that has become a stronghold created in the mind. We need the power of God to break free of that barrier and way of thinking. That's why when we are in Christ, we are commanded to be transformed by the renewing of our minds! Transformation cannot take place when we still harbour the same old destructive thought patterns. An non-renewed mind will always cause problems in a our life affecting relationships and everything pertaining to life. Refusing to adjust and change our way of thinking blocks progress and stunts growth. Our own thoughts can be our worst enemy!

The Word of God is the perfect guide on how we ought to think of ourselves. What God calls me is what I call myself and how I perceive myself. What I think of myself is never influenced by what others think of me. I forge my own destiny by the principles in the Word of God!

Channel Your Thoughts in a Positive Direction

Man is made or unmade by himself; in the "armoury" of thought he forges the weapons by which he destroys himself. He also fashions the tools with which he builds for himself heavenly mansions of joy and strength and peace.
—James Allen

As beings of power, intelligence, and love, the lords of our own thoughts, we hold the key to every situation, and we contain within ourselves that transforming and regenerative agency by which we may make ourselves what we will. I believe that everyone is born in this world with the same measure and capacity to attain "riches and wealth". (I'm not just talking about money and material things but also about health, a sound mind, and everything that pertains to having a good life and enjoying it.) The only difference is how we channel our thoughts to gravitate towards that which God has already given us the power to have. Whilst it is of great benefit to the giver, to gracefully receive when given, don't have a mindset of receiving only, but be a generous giver too. Make a list of what you desire in life, confess it every day, and then start giving generously. Write down precisely what you intend to give in return for that which you desire in life! You could have everything you want in life if only you would help enough other people get their desires met as well.

Everything you will ever achieve, and everything you will fail to achieve, is a direct result of your own thought patterns. You attract what you secretly harbour in your heart, what you love, and what you fear. If you don't like the things that have been following you, check what you have been either desiring or fearing in the confines of your soul! You do not attract what you want but what you are, and your thoughts helped shape who you are! Improve your life by improving your thought pattern! Don't be stuck in destructive thought cycles! When you speak of your negative circumstances (poverty, lack of education, race barrier, etc.), you are simply directing your mind's power to attract these undesirable circumstances. It is true that whatever your mind feeds upon, your mind attracts. Always understand that thoughts are spiritual. It is critical that you only think of the things that are true, honest, just, pure, lovely, of good report, virtuous, and praiseworthy. Improve the quality of your life by improving the quality of your thoughts. Now measure your thought patterns with the above-mentioned eight attributes that contribute to a healthy thought life and a positive life in general. Use these eight characteristics to determine how you choose to think of others as well. Are your thoughts towards the next person true, honest, just, pure, lovely, of good report, virtuous, and praiseworthy? Think about it, because what you think about yourself and others has the power to transform your life. It's all a matter of choice. Make the right choices and think the right thoughts! Let your thoughts bring light into your spirit. Where there was darkness, let it dissipate. Let your thoughts be praiseworthy, rooted in God's truth, and infused with Godly imagination.

A man cannot directly choose his circumstances, but he can choose his thoughts, and so indirectly, yet surely, shape his circumstances.
—James Allen

MUSIC, LITERATURE, IMAGES

A noble and Godlike character is not a thing of favour or chance, but is the natural result of continued effort in right thinking, the effect of long-cherished association with Godlike thoughts.
—James Allen

Music: Sometimes it's worth stating the obvious, because the obvious might not be so obvious to the next person. The type of music we listen to can influence us consciously and subconsciously. It's interesting how our memory can register a song subconsciously, even without much of our attention to the song. Music is one of the greatest influences among young people. The type of music we listen to can influence our behavioural patterns and have psychological effects. Music influences our mind and thoughts, behaviour, emotions, and overall mood. When we are sad and you put on an upbeat or groovy song, the sound sends impulses to our brain that make us feel happy. The opposite is also true; music can affect our emotions and make us cry. Music has got the power to even make us rebellious. It is all related to the impulses that are being sent to the brain through the style (type) of music and lyrical content.

What do you spend your time listening to and feeding your soul? Listen to the right type of music for positive stimulation of the mind.

Literature and Images: The kind of material we read or study has got the same effect on the brain and our thought life. What we allow our eyes to see (images) is actually planted into our conscious and subconscious memory as well. At times we find that even our dreams can reflect what we've been feeding our mind on, through magazines, the Internet and so forth. Watch out for what enters your heart either through your eyes (eye gates) or your ears (ear gates). It's time to eliminate the junk and start feeding your soul with the right food.

In conclusion to this principle, watch your thoughts. You are where you are today because of your thoughts first and then your words. Channel your thoughts in the right direction and enjoy liberation of the mind. When you free your mind, you free yourself to go wherever your mind desires and directs you. Feed and nourish your mind with the right information and healthy thoughts. The call is yours.

POWER NOTES:

Man is the master of thought, the moulder of character, and maker and sharper of condition, environment, and destiny! —James Allen

Your mind is the master weaver, both of the inner garment of character, and the outer garment of circumstance. —James Allen

Act is the blossom of thought, and joy and suffering are its fruits; thus does a man garner in the sweet and bitter fruitage of his own husbandry. —James Allen

Prayer: I ask not oh divine providence, for more riches, but more wisdom with which to accept and use wisely the riches I received at birth in the form of the power to control and direct my mind to whatever ends I desire —Napoleon Hill

Philippians 4:8
King James Version (KJV)

Finally, brethren, whatsoever things are true, whatsoever things are honest, whatsoever things are just, whatsoever things are pure, whatsoever things are lovely, whatsoever things are of good report; if there be any virtue, and if there be any praise, think on these things.

The Magic of Thinking Big
David Schwartz

- *You are what you think you are.*
- *Believe you can succeed, and you will.*
- *Action cures fear, always take the first initiative.*
- *Think progress, believe progress, and push progress.*
- *Study setbacks to pave your way to success.*
- *Be a doer, and not a don't-er.*
- *Give spiritual strength to people, and they will give genuine affection to you.*
- *Manage your environment, go first class.*
- *Use the big thinker's vocabulary, and use big, bright, and cheerful words!*
- *Tune into channel P (for positive), the good and healthy thoughts station.*

Purpose in your heart to think and breed positive thoughts only!

Principle #5:

WATCH YOUR WORDS

*Words have got power, presence, prophetic
implication and no geographical limitation.*
—Dr Cindy Trimm

James 3:5–12
Amplified Bible (AMP)

*Even so the tongue is a little member, and it can boast of great things.
See how much wood or how great a forest a tiny spark can set ablaze!
And the tongue is a fire. [The tongue is a] world of wickedness
set among our members, contaminating and depraving the
whole body and setting on fire the wheel of birth (the cycle of
man's nature), being itself ignited by hell (Gehenna).
For every kind of beast and bird, of reptile and sea animal, can
be tamed and has been tamed by human genius (nature).
But the human tongue can be tamed by no man. It is a restless
(undisciplined, irreconcilable) evil, full of deadly poison.
With it we bless the Lord and Father, and with it we
curse men who were made in God's likeness!
Out of the same mouth come forth blessing and cursing.
These things, my brethren, ought not to be so.
Does a fountain send forth [simultaneously] from
the same opening fresh water and bitter?
Can a fig tree, my brethren, bear olives, or a grapevine
figs? Neither can a salt spring furnish fresh water.*

Moving on from thoughts, we come to confession, because what you think becomes what you eventually profess on almost a daily basis. What comes out of your mouth is determined by what goes into your mind. Just like thoughts, your words also help shape and frame your world. What words do you speak over your life, family, children, friends, associates, and so forth. Think about this: Do the words you speak bring life or the opposite? Are your words helping build others up or destroying them? What do you allow to come out of your mouth at any given time? Are you too loose with your words? Because when you come to think of it, most of us are too liberal with our words and that has cost us! Is your tongue a wellspring of life, or is it a wellspring of death? Words, words, words, words – how costly they are if spoken unwisely!

Proverbs 6:2

Amplified Bible (AMP)
*You are snared with the words of your lips, you
are caught by the speech of your mouth.*

Just like with thoughts, some of us are stuck in cycles of failure and bad habits because of our words, because what you think eventually becomes what you confess, and like thoughts, what you confess with your mouth becomes reality. Words create "a thing"; when you confess or speak something with your own mouth, you give it permission to exist. I'm asking, What are you creating with your words? A lot of us have become ensnared by the words we speak. If you don't want to see something appearing in your future, then don't say it. Don't give it permission to exist by confessing it and believing it, especially if it's a lie and meant to sabotage or destroy your life or someone else's. Your words also frame your world!

Proverbs 12:14

Amplified Bible (AMP)
*From the fruit of his words a man shall be satisfied with good, and
the work of a man's hands shall come back to him [as a harvest].*

The Bible says in proverbs 12:14, "From the fruit of his words, a man shall be satisfied with good" Yes, your words yield forth fruit. Good and positive constructive words produce good fruit, and negative, destructive words produce after their own kind. Positive words will *never* produce bad fruit, and negative words will *never* produce good fruit. So don't be deceived. The Bible says in Galatians 6:7, "For whatever (emphasis on whatever) a man sows, that he will also reap." What words are you sowing, either in your own life or other people's lives? For example, every time you confess that you are broke, then forever broke shall you be, unless you undo that cycle of lack by starting to confess the positive. My father taught me to always say, "I'm temporarily out of cash", whenever I was low on finances. He taught the same principle to everyone around him, and this is true, because your lack of finances is only temporary. It's never meant to last. Speak yourself out of lack right now, and believe in your heart the positive words you confess. It's time we start calling the things that are not as if they were, just like the Word of God advises us.

Thou Shall Not Complain

Be grateful, the attitude of gratitude is by far the most important attitude which we could ever acquire in life. The more you express gratitude for what you have, the more you will have to express gratitude for. Happiness isn't about getting what you want all the time, it's about loving what you have and being grateful for it.

—Zig Ziglar

Complaining aggravates a situation; it impedes progress. The children of Israel took forty years on a journey that could have taken them eleven days to complete (according to research). Why? They complained, moaned, groaned, and doubted God. Hence, the first generation of Israel to come out of Egypt did not see the Promised Land! Don't be caught in the same trap. Some of us are stuck in the same unproductive, unfruitful cycles because of complaining. You complain about everything and anything: I don't like my job, my children are a nightmare, I'm too short, I'm too tall, they don't care about me, I don't like going to school—the list is endless! The more you complain, the more miserable you are, and the less you enjoy God's promises. Those in camp complaining are always miserable, yet they need to realise that they are the solution to their misery. Snap out of it, look on the positive side, and enjoy God's abundant blessing. The fact that you are breathing is a blessing, so enjoy the gift of being able to inhale and exhale air!

My brother can't stand people who complain; it's like you are pricking him with thorns whenever you complain around him. He can tolerate you to a certain extent but is sure to correct you in a way that will silence your complaints or make you change your course of conversation into a more positive one. I totally understand him. Why? Complainers are a pain to be around. Now think about it: if we as humans react like this, what about God Himself?

Instead of complaining, why not think of something pleasant to be thankful about? There are many reasons to be thankful: your good health, your job (some don't have one), your friends, your family, even life itself (because you are alive!).

Instead of complaints, let your mouth be filled with praise. Force it out of you if you have to. Start speaking positively about the situations that might have previously caused you to complain.

In The Image of God

Genesis 1:26

Amplified Bible (AMP)

God said, Let Us [Father, Son, and Holy Spirit] make mankind in Our image, after Our likeness, and let them have complete authority over the fish of the sea, the birds of the air, the [tame] beasts, and over all of the earth, and over everything that creeps upon the earth.

Image: A representation of a person or thing, a visual impression of something in a lens, mirror, and so forth.

Likeness: Having the same characteristics, similar, equal,; appearance, form, and resemblance.

Sometimes the obvious terms are not so obvious, so I had to find the proper meanings of the two above terms. The Bible clearly states that we are made in the *image* of God, and after His *likeness.* This simply means we are God-like and therefore should possess the same characteristics as our Father in heaven. We are like a representation of Him, and this shows me that if my Father in heaven spoke the world into existence by the power of His Word, then I have the same power to speak something into existence—because I'm made in His image, after His likeness, right? If only people fully understood this concept, then you would think twice before you spoke! You say your world is in a mess, but I say, you created that mess for yourself by the words you spoke. Please understand this: that we have the same creative power through our words as our Heavenly Father does. Now see this:

Genesis 1
Amplified Bible (AMP)

³ *And "God said"*, let there be light; and there was light.

⁶ *And "God said"*, Let there be a firmament [the expanse of the sky] in the midst of the waters, and let it separate the waters [below] from the waters [above].

⁹ *And "God said"*, Let the waters under the heavens be collected into one place [of standing], and let the dry land appear. And it was so.

¹¹ *And "God said"*, let the earth put forth [tender] vegetation: plants yielding seed and fruit trees yielding fruit whose seed is in itself, each according to its kind, upon the earth. And it was so.

¹⁴ *And "God said"*, Let there be lights in the expanse of the heavens to separate the day from the night, and let them be signs *and* tokens [of God's provident care], and [to mark] seasons, days, and years,

²⁰And "God said", Let the waters bring forth abundantly *and* swarm with living creatures, and let birds fly over the earth in the open expanse of the heavens.

²²And "God blessed them, saying", be fruitful, multiply, and fill the waters in the seas, and let the fowl multiply in the earth.

²⁴And "God said", let the earth bring forth living creatures according to their kinds: livestock, creeping things, and [wild] beasts of the earth according to their kinds. And it was so.

²⁶ "God said", Let Us [Father, Son, and Holy Spirit] make mankind in Our image, after Our likeness, and let them have complete authority over the fish of the sea, the birds of the air, the [tame] beasts, and over all of the earth, and over everything that creeps upon the earth.

²⁸And "God blessed them and said to them", Be fruitful, multiply, and fill the earth, and subdue it [using all its vast resources in the service of God and man]; and have dominion over the fish of the sea, the birds of the air, and over every living creature that moves upon the earth.

This is to show you God's creative power at work through the words He spoke during creation. Now that should speak volumes to us, especially if we understand that we are made in His image, and after His likeness! Every time God spoke something, it was created; He gave it permission to exist! What are you giving permission to exist in your world? God *said* and then *there was*. If God created the world using words, what about us who were made in His image and after His likeness?

Scenario:
Mandy is a mother, and every day she tells her daughter Cora that she'll never amount to anything, that she is lazy and good for nothing.
So when her book of life is written, it will also go like this:

And Mandy said, "My daughter Cora will never amount to anything", and it was so. Her daughter grew up being lazy and good for nothing indeed, just like her mother had spoken over her life!

Now, unless if somebody enlightens and educates Cora, she will never know the power that she has to undo the negative words spoken over her life by her own mother. Indeed, she will be lazy, and her thought pattern will be reflected by how filthy and disorganised her environment will be. Don't prevent your own children's progress and success by the words you speak over them. What words are you writing into your children's futures? Parents, learn to bless your children; a good father blesses his children. Speak into them what you would desire to see them become in life. Be the prophet of your own house and your own life and prophesy.

What Is Your Name?

I thank God for my mother Mary. She always called me a king, and that gave me confidence and helped shape who I am today. She saw potential in me and spoke it into my life; what a wise mother! And not only that, but I was even given the name David to affirm what my parents saw in me from the moment I was born! And we all know who David was from the Bible: he was a king, a musician, a man after God's own heart, and a prophet. My name also means "beloved"; that explains why I'm unconditionally loved dearly, beyond human comprehension. That also explains my passion for music, and my love for God. Hahaha, don't get me excited now, because I can go on with this knowledge in my very own name! Parents, naming your child is very important. The name you give them can either break them or propel them toward destiny. A child's name will always associate them with their character and behaviour, unless that name is changed! Think wisely before you name them. The book of Proverbs says, "A good name is better than precious ointment." This Scripture has got two sides to it: name as in birth name, and name as in reputation. There's a direct link between the two, because as I said, the name you carry affects your character and behaviour. For example, the name Barrington means "a troublesome tribe or a troublesome person." The person with that kind of name will live up to it.

The same goes for the name Anthony, an aristocratic name meaning "worthy of praise or admiration." So I ask again, what is your name?

When I came to this knowledge about names and behaviour, I had to quickly do some research to find out what my name meant; if there were any negative stigmas attached to it, I was ready to change it myself!

If you notice, in the Bible God had to change some people's names, too. I'll list just a few examples:

> **Abraham**: At first, he was called Abram. God had to change his name to Abraham, which means "father of many". Having the correct name was important to God, because the name would carry the *essence* (intrinsic nature, quintessence, nature, spirit, life, heart, and substance) of his whole being. It would reaffirm his purpose and destiny and seal the covenant he had with God as a father of many, who carried kings and nations in his loins. His greatness was engrafted into his name and DNA, together with Sarah. (Read Genesis 17:5–16)

> **Sarah:** Sarah's name was originally Sarai. But God had to change it to complement Abraham's name, since she was his wife. Her name had to support God's vision for Abraham and the Children of Israel. Nations and kings were to come from her as well. (Genesis 17:5–16)

> **Israel:** Before he was called Israel, his name was Jacob. Jacob meant "holder of the heel" or "supplanter", which means a deceiver, or one who overthrows someone on purpose, or a usurper. He surely lived up to his name until God changed his name to Israel. Israel can be translated as "to "wrestle with God"; some commentators argue that also means to rule, to be strong, to have authority over. Either way, God changed his name for a purpose! (Read Genesis 32:28–29)

Gideon: With the case of Gideon, it was more of a name addition rather than name change. He was given the name Jerub-baal, which means "let Baal (the Evil One) contend with him", since he tore down an altar of the false god Baal. Other translations say "destroyer of the evil one". The name Gideon itself means "he that bruises or breaks", a destroyer. Some translations go on to say "mighty warrior". This explains why the angel would address him as "mighty man of valour." When he was hiding from his enemies, the angel of the Lord had to remind him and reaffirm the meaning of his name so that he could live up to it in the face of fear.

The wrong name can alter God's purpose for your life. It can make you gravitate towards the wrong destiny if not changed! When people call your name, they continually affirm and reinforce that name and the meaning behind it. Some of us need to undo what has been negatively spoken over us, either through the names we carry or just negative words in general. Identify the areas in your life where progress is impeded and start undoing what has been set in motion. It's now time to start recalibrating your world by speaking positive words and creating a positive atmosphere all around you.

Have Dominion; Take Charge of the Day

Sometime we forget that God instructed us to be fruitful and multiply. We were instructed to have "dominion". We should be productive (fruitful) and should be living as rulers rather than subjects of our environments. A lot of us have forgotten our true identity and are living as slaves to our natural or spiritual circumstances. We cry over anything and everything, and yet God gave us the mandate to be in control and take charge. Now here is what the word dominion means:

Meaning 1: *Sovereignty or control*
Synonyms: Supremacy, ascendancy, domination, superiority, dominance, pre-eminence, primacy, authority, mastery, control, command, power, rule, lordship, leadership, power, and influence.

Meaning 2: *The territory of a sovereign or government*
Synonyms: Synonyms: dependency, colony, territory, province, outpost, satellite, holding, possession, realm, kingdom, empire, domain, country, nation land, and so forth.

Don't you know that God made you sovereign over your own environment? And your environment is your territory. It's your kingdom, your province, your territory, and you are meant to have dominion over it rather than the other way round. Your circumstances and everything about you – your personage, possessions, property, job, etc. – all fall into your territory. Be the one to be in charge and have dominion by speaking words that bring life into your kingdom.

Every time when you wake up in the morning, make it a habit to speak positive words into your day, into the atmosphere, into your environment, into your territory, and believe those words in your heart. Call the things that you want to happen in your day, take charge of the day, take charge of your environment, of your kingdom, of your territory; take command and allow the Holy Spirit to guide you. I often hear people complaining about Mondays. Personally, I've never had a bad Monday; all I know is that just like any other day, it is the day that the Lord has made, and I make the choice to rejoice and be glad in the day. The moment you wake up with such a positive attitude, and the moment you speak positivity in the day, you find that you enjoy the day. Instead of complaining and whining about Mondays, why not thank God for allowing you to see a brand new day, because some did not make it into the day. I also say this of every new year, each time God allows you to see a new year. Bless every 1st of January, speak what you would want to see in the year, command everything to come into alignment, declare the year is yours and everything works in your favour. Speak into your kingdom like the king you were meant to be. You are your own prophet. You don't have to be a prophet to prophesy into your own life or your family's life. Why not take a stand and start declaring what you want to see over your life, family, friends, businesses, health, finances, etc.? Why not declare your home blessed, declare your family blessed, declare your finances blessed, declare your friends blessed. (Mention them by their full names, too, so that the blessing goes to the right postcode!) Extract every promise in the Word of God and declare it over your life and over other people's lives.

Recalibrate Your Environment

Job 22:28

New King James Version (NKJV)

You will also declare a thing, and it will be established for you: so light will shine on your ways.

Meaning of recalibrate: To alter or change.
Synonyms: Adapt, adjust, amend, change, convert, correct mid-course, develop, dial back, diversify, doctor, fine tune, make different, metamorphose, modify, mutate, reconstruct, renovate, refashion, remodel, reshape, shift, transform, and turn.
Antonyms: Fix, continue, keep, let stand, sustain, retain, and remain

It's time for the weak to now say *"I am strong"*, the poor to say *"I am rich"*, and the ill to declare *"I am healed"* – not *I shall be*, but *I am*, as in the present continuous tense. Declare in the *now*! Never go before God with the problem. You magnify it before His presence, but speak and declare the answer, pray the solution, pray the results you want to see, and believe. Use God's Word to your advantage; take Him at His Word. You see, for every negative situation, there is always a counteraction through the Word of God. Instead of speaking fear, declare Luke 10:19; instead of continuously talking about your illness, declare Isaiah 53:5. The Word of God is full of promises for us and is an effective weapon to fire against every enemy of life. Learn the Scriptures. Declare His promises aloud, and let your words impact every atom in your environment through your voice exerting pressure against every element that has come against you. Your words carry weight and force, especially when the power of belief is added to them.

I have drafted an example of how you could recalibrate your environment just by speaking into the atmosphere. A lot of us need to adjust, alter, change, amend, and fine-tune our environment so that we can change the course of our lives into a positive direction. Don't just say something once and then expect instant change. Your words (just like thoughts) are like seeds planted; keep cultivating and watering the seed through persistent declaration until what you speak and desire becomes reality, until the words that you speak come to fruition. That's why Jesus encouraged us to "pray without ceasing". Pray until something happens. As you declare these words, remember this: God has ordained you as a king here on earth, and from my understanding, the Word of the king is a command, a declaration that has to be obeyed by the forces of nature and everything that pertains to your life. We are made in His image, so take up your priestly and royal role with authority, boldly declare, and light will shine in your path. What I know about light is that where there is true light, there is order. Declare, and let there be light in your environment! Arise, shine, for the glory of the Lord has risen upon thee. Command everything around you, and everything about you, to fall into place and align with destiny.

DAILY CONFESSIONS

Thank you, Lord, for yet another day. Thank you for the power and authority you have invested in me to take charge and command of my day and my surroundings. You have given me dominion, and therefore In the name of Jesus Christ I declare these things:

- ❖ According to Jeremiah 33:3, I call unto you and you answer me. You show me great and mighty things which I know not of.
- ❖ This is the day you have made, I rejoice and I'm glad in it.
- ❖ This is my day and everything shifts in my favour.
- ❖ I am forgiven of all my sin, and my transgressions are blotted out. I release and forgive everyone who has ever wronged me or hurt me. I choose to forgive right now and I release any feelings of bitterness, anger and resentment. I am at peace.
- ❖ I wait in great anticipation of the things you have in store for me, and I receive all you have prepared for me for this day called today.
- ❖ I speak positivity, progress, and success into the day. Every element of the day cooperates with my destiny and the words that I release into the atmosphere. The sound that I release from my voice calibrates my atmosphere into what I speak into it!
- ❖ You arise over me and Your glory is seen upon me. Gentiles come to my light, and kings to the brightness of my rising. (According to Isaiah 60:1–3)
- ❖ You make me radiant and make my heart swell with joy. You convert the abundance of the sea to me, and You grant unto me the wealth of the Gentiles. (Isaiah 60:5)
- ❖ I denounce and nullify any diabolical (devilish, demonic, evil) subverting activity against my businesses, family, friends, associates, my own life, and anything that concerns me. I declare that no weapon formed against me shall prosper, and according to Luke 10:19, nothing will harm me, for you have given me authority to trample on snakes and scorpions (demonic forces) and to overcome all the wiles or tactics of the enemy.
- ❖ There shall be no satanic encroachment or any demonic squatters to be found in my life and territory! Father, by your power, and by the finger of God, I command the enemy to get his hands off my life, possessions and property, and family. Whatever belongs to me burns the enemy's hands by the blood of Jesus Christ! I denounce and render powerless the spirit of witchcraft, and I speak destruction and confusion into the enemy's camp. Let

the blood of Jesus Christ, the fire of the Holy Ghost, and your angels form hedges and walls of protection all over my life, and all over everything and anyone connected to me!

❖ I reverse and veto any contrivance (stratagem, trick, or plot) of the enemy against my life and anybody connected with me. Father, put the enemy's tactics to shame, and rid me of every evil and ill word spoken against my family, friends, or myself, and anything that concerns me. Every evil word spoken – I render it powerless and futile. Bridle the tongues and lips of my enemies, cause their hearts to fail. (Enemies mentioned here are not people; we attack the spirit behind them. So show no mercy to any spirit that has stood in your way and against your purpose.)

❖ Jehovah Gibbor, Jehovah Sabbaoth, thank you for assigning your angels to watch over me and lift me up in their hands, and for standing up for my help, lest I dash my feet against a stone. I will not fear. Because of you, my enemies are subdued and confounded; they are put to shame. (Psalm 91)

❖ You rid me of every character assassin; the anointing upon my life repels such. According to Numbers 10:35, You arise in my life and my enemies are scattered.

❖ I will not be a conduit for the enemy's tactics and plans. Every door that might have been open to the enemy, Father, shut it right now! I refuse to be the weak link! My soul does not waver; it is firmly fixed and rooted in You.

❖ The anointing upon my life breaks the yoke of the Evil One.

❖ I am more than a conqueror, and nothing shall separate me from the love of Christ. Father, superimpose your will over my life, and over my family. Dismantle the enemy's plans and ploys, for Your name's sake!

❖ I have a good name and a good reputation. I am unconditionally loved, and I unconditionally release love back as well.

❖ The blessing of Abraham is my portion.

❖ I am out of debt, and thank you for granting unto me finance management skills and investment strategies.

❖ I am the head and never the tail.

❖ I am above and never beneath.

❖ I am blessed and highly favoured, and never cursed. Thank you for letting Your favour prevail towards me as you did with Daniel.

❖ I am full of wisdom, knowledge, and understanding. I take captive my thoughts and declare that they are totally surrendered to the influence of Your Word.

❖ I break through barriers and limitations.

❖ I have acute spiritual insight.

❖ All things work together for my good, because I love You and I'm called according to Your perfect will and purpose.

❖ I speak into my day and command everything (including my mind) to align with Your divine purpose and will for my life.

❖ I am the apple of Your eye, wonderfully and fearfully made.

❖ I am like a green olive tree in the house of God; I trust in the mercies of God forever.

❖ My family, friends, associates, and everybody connected to me are blessed.

❖ You came that I might enjoy life, and have it in abundance. Therefore I declare that I have life in abundance, and I live to my maximum potential. I am pregnant with purpose, visions, and dreams that come to fruition.

❖ I am healthy and physically fit, and my mind is sound.

❖ By the stripes of Jesus Christ I am healed from every sickness, illness, infirmity, and destructive addictions. Every generational and degenerative disease is severed by the blood of Christ! In Christ Jesus I am free!

❖ You pour the oil of joy over me and clothe me with the garment of praise.

❖ I am a citizen of the kingdom of heaven, an ambassador of Christ, the light of the world.

❖ According to Ephesians 2:6, I'm seated in heavenly places in Christ Jesus!

❖ I am the salt of the earth.

- ❖ I am an influencer, and I leave an enduring legacy which lasts throughout generations.
- ❖ Everything about me is blessed; everything I do and touch prospers.
- ❖ My business ideas and plans come to fruition. I do not abort vision, dreams, and purpose. I am not a quitter! When the winds come raging, thank You for strength to endure the pressure and testing and to come out a winner like the champion I am.
- ❖ My set time of favour will not be frustrated.
- ❖ I am full of Your Word, and it illuminates my path.
- ❖ You are my Shepherd, and I shall not want. (We might as well declare the whole of Psalm 23). I thank You because You are my shield and exceeding great reward.
- ❖ My mouth is filled with Your praise, worship, thanksgiving, adoration, and blessing.
- ❖ You came that I might enjoy life and have it in abundance, and You also promised that those who believe in You will not perish but have everlasting life. Therefore I declare that I will not perish, my family will not perish, my health will not perish, my finances will not perish. I declare that there is light and life all around me and no confusion!
- ❖ You bless me and keep me. You make Your face to shine upon me and are gracious towards me. You lift up your countenance towards me and bless me with peace.

In Jesus Christ's name, I declare everything I've confessed comes to pass. Father, I believe in my heart every word I've spoken, and I receive the answer to every declaration right now. You promised in Your Word that if I believe in my heart, then I shall receive whatever I ask for in Your name. And whatever I think or say, it shall be established according to my faith; so let it be according to Your Word and promise.

Amen

Now, I've listed these declarations as an example; feel free to adopt them in your daily prayer life. But don't be too lazy to make up your own list and expand on what I've written down. Search the Scriptures and draft a list of declarations. In conclusion to this principle, watch your words, because they have power, presence, prophetic implication, and no geographical limitation. What you speak and confess will follow you wherever you go, even if you decide to move out of country! You might not see a thing manifest immediately after it's confessed, but trust me, the seed has been planted, and it's only a matter of time before the fruit is borne.

Purpose in your heart to watch the words that come out of your mouth!

Principle #6:

HAVE FAITH

Anything is possible to him that believes.
–Jesus Christ

What Is Faith?

Hebrews 11:1
Amplified Bible (AMP)

Now faith is the assurance (the confirmation, the title deed) of the things [we] hope for, being the proof of things [we] do not see and the conviction of their reality [faith perceiving as real fact what is not revealed to the senses].

The King James Version calls faith the substance of things hoped for. It's the belief in, or evidence of the things not "seen", or revealed to the "natural" senses as the amplified further explains. I liken faith to a coin with two sides:

a) The *trust* in God and His power – believing that He can do exceedingly, abundantly, and beyond what you can think or imagine. Faith is the power of belief!

b) The *existence* of God – believing that He is, and that He is a rewarder of them that diligently seek Him.

Faith is the currency in heaven's endless supply. When you have this coin of faith, you are richer than the richest person; you are unstoppable, and you have access to a world of endless supply, because your success is not determined by what you see with the natural eye. The natural eye is short-sighted, only functioning with the immediate environment. It is but limited, and cannot see beyond obstacles. It does not have the capability to "*beam*" through a barrier, but stops and gives up when there's a stumbling block in its path. But the eye of faith goes beyond the natural, beyond your immediate environment and into realms of untapped potential. Note that the Bible says that without this currency called faith, without this "coin", without this "eye" that sees beyond the natural, it is *impossible* to please God the King. And the Bible also says that we walk not by sight (what we see in our present circumstances) but by faith (2 Corinthians 5:7). This encourages us to call the things that are not as if they were. What is seen is only temporary, but what is not seen is eternal. Your faith gives you access to the supernatural. It is the force that makes you through prayer, pull resources from the kingdom of heaven (the Spirit realm), down into the natural realm. The Spirit realm is the causal realm; this is where things happen first, before they impact the natural realm. Everything we see in our natural world is a mirror of the spiritual world. Many are blind to this truth because they have become so accustomed to the natural realm which they can see with their physical eyes, and which their physical senses are so familiar with.

The natural realm is but limited. The truth is, the spiritual realm is much more real and much bigger than our natural world. Our faith makes us tap into the things of the Spirit and live by them instead of depending on the flesh, which is limiting! You can never understand spiritual matters with a natural mind. If your senses are not attuned to the spiritual realm, you will never understand the things of God, because God is Spirit, and those who worship Him must worship in Spirit and in Truth (John 4:24). When you have received the Spirit and live by the Spirit, then you have found the truth, and you live in truth because the Spirit reveals that which pertains to life (the spiritual; John 16:13)! For faith to be effective, it is important that your body and soul (your psyche, reasoning, emotion, and desire) be in sync with the Spirit. Anybody can believe, but not everyone can walk in the faith of spiritual conviction. Think about it! When spiritual conviction takes over, you do not need proof to believe desired results. As a matter of fact, you have confidence in the results before there is proof.

You can pray for twenty-four hours a day and fast four times a week, but without faith being married to your prayer, all is in vain. For it is only your faith that moves God – not the amount of tears that you shed when faced with trouble, and certainly not your many words before His presence.

- Faith believes in the creative and delivering power of God. It believes in all the attributes attached to His name (*Jireh, Rapha, Shalom, Nissi*), so that whenever we have a need, the All-Sufficient One manifests the attribute that is suited to that need.
- Faith believes in God's Word and patiently awaits His promises enshrined within it.
- Faith takes God at His Word!
- Faith believes in the holiness of God and abstains from offending the King. Faith makes you approach His throne with boldness, believing you obtain mercy and favour from the King.
- Faith opens the pathway to your answer through its powerful force.
- Faith is the light that beams and cannot be hidden when surrounded with total darkness.
- Faith seeks after the heart of God and endeavours to execute His plans.
- Faith should be fasting and prayer's companion.
- Faith believes in the delivering power of God, knowing that all things are possible with God, nothing is too hard or impossible for Him, and that all things work together for the good to them that love and believe the Lord and are called according to is perfect purpose (Matthew 19:26).

Matthew 17:20
Amplified Bible (AMP)

He said to them, Because of the littleness of your faith [that is, your lack of firmly relying trust]. For truly I say to you, if you have faith [that is living] like a grain of mustard seed, you can say to this mountain, Move from here to yonder place, and it will move; and nothing will be impossible to you.

Have you ever noticed how Jesus would question the depth of his disciples' faith? Every time He was displeased with their faith, He would protest, "O ye of little faith". The Bible also declares that if you have faith as little as a mustard seed you can tell a mountain to move, and it will move! Why the mustard seed? It is one of the tiniest of seeds and yet produces the biggest results; it grows to be the biggest of all garden plants! Even when planted underneath a boulder, it has the potential to crack the rock and find its way up to the surface. The mustard seed is not affected by its surroundings, and neither should your faith be. Your faith should remain fixed and unmovable. Those that are planted in the Lord shall never be moved, even when the storms rage, even when the tempest of winds blow, even when passing through a dry land. Whatever the circumstances, their faith remains firmly fixed! Have vision like an eagle, which stays focused on its prey until it grabs it. Remain focused ahead, no matter what obstacles come your way, and eventually you will succeed. Unwavering faith always produces positive results.

The Power of Belief: Faith vs. Fear and Doubt

Mark 11:24
New King James Version (NKJV)

Therefore I say to you, whatever things you ask when you pray, believe that you receive them, and you will have them.

Anything is possible to him that believes. This takes us back to the principle of thinking. Your belief system has power over you and your environment. If your mind can conceive a thing, and believe it, results are imminent. It all goes back to the mind and your thoughts! When your belief system is set on the positive side, no situation is impossible or impassable for you, especially if you know the One whom you serve! For those who trust in Him shall never be put to shame, as His Word declares. With Him, all things are possible; just believe. Before Jesus healed one woman we read about in Scripture, He asked her if she believed that she could be made whole. The woman said yes, and it was so according to her faith. Jesus always responded to people's faith, and in places where there was no faith, He couldn't do many miracles.

Jeremiah 17:7–8
Amplified Bible (AMP)

*[Most] blessed is the man who believes in, trusts in, and relies
on the Lord, and whose hope and confidence the Lord is.
For he shall be like a tree planted by the waters that spreads out
its roots by the river; and it shall not see and fear when heat
comes; but its leaf shall be green. It shall not be anxious and full
of care in the year of drought, nor shall it cease yielding fruit.*

Fear and doubt are the products of lack of faith. When you lose faith, when you give away your power to believe, that empty space is occupied with fear and doubt. Once you start to doubt, once you allow yourself to become afraid, you have already lost your faith, because both cannot coexist and produce positive results; one has to give way to the other. Fear is not of God, because He has given us a spirit of power, love, and a sound mind. When you give way to fear, you lose your personal power and authority. The way you love others is affected (for perfect love casteth out fear). There's no way you can be afraid and have a sound mind at the same time, because when you have fear, your mind is never sound; it is scattered! Refuse to be afraid, have faith, and stand your ground, even when faced with adversity. Fear always has a tendency to exaggerate a situation, presenting it as giant before you. But be bold, and rise up like David when he was faced with Goliath. When the so-called "trained army" of Saul became afraid and shrieked with fear at the sight of Goliath, David arose with boldness and faced the "uncircumcised Philistine" (this represents things not even worth crying over, posing as giants before you) who dared defy the armies of the living God. Watch the faith that David demonstrated even in the words he confessed (1 Samuel 17:45–47). His attitude secured victory for him because he had the right paradigm and believed God without a doubt. Victory for David was sweet. People ended up ascribing more greatness to David than to Saul, because David conquered the so-called "giant" that had brought terror to Israel. What giants are you facing? Whatever giant it is, it can be conquered with the right attitude of faith!

Consider when Jesus gave Peter the invitation to walk on water: Peter started off with the right attitude as he walked on water for a few minutes. The only moment he started to sink was when he entertained the wrong thoughts and lost focus on Christ (his goal). He looked at the waves and became afraid, instead of keeping his focus on Jesus and trusting His Word to simply *come*. Fear brings false imaginations into reality. Don't entertain it. No wonder God says "Fear not" over eighty times in the Bible. Fear cripples you; it constricts and suffocates potential. Resist it! Have the "John 5:8 faith" that causes you to pick up your mat and walk. Like the crippled man by the pool, for so many years you have been stuck in cycles of fear and failure, but now is the time you come out of your disability and follow the voice of Jesus telling you to rise up and start walking! Worry and fear block the hand of God from moving. That's why Jesus commanded us not to worry or to be entangled in the cares and stresses of life, but instead to trust God for our welfare.

Faith Without Works Is Dead:
Have you bought the lotto ticket?
—Munashe Chibwe

Imagine going before God and asking Him to help you win the lotto. Day in, day out, you pray without ceasing, going before His throne with boldness believing that He will answer your prayer and help you win the lotto. You even ask others to help you pray regarding the issue. You are so eager to win the lotto! You see others winning, and then deep in your heart you ask God when your turn will come. But then I ask you one question: *Have you actually bought the lotto ticket so that you can register for a chance to win?*

Does this scenario sound familiar? Could that be you in that position? Most of us ask and ask God to do something. Yes, we have the right attitude when we go before Him, but He will ask you the same question: Have you bought your ticket? What work will you produce before Him as evidence of your belief in what you are asking for? Rather than just asking and waiting for God to give the answer, He says, "Get up and start working towards the answer you desire!" – because remember, Jesus promised that whatsoever we ask in His name we shall have, as long as we believe. Don't just ask for God to bless you with financial breakthrough and then sit and do nothing but wait for an answer; get up and start looking for a job, or start a business. That's when God will intervene and open the doors necessary for you to prosper in that which you have asked for from Him.

I know of a couple who really wanted a baby boy after having three girls. They went for a scan, but according to hospital policy, they could not be told the supposed sex of the baby; it would have to be revealed when the child was born. So the mother stepped out in faith. She went and started buying baby boy clothes, and even when she spoke to family members and friends, she would tell them to buy only baby boy clothes, because she firmly believed that she was going to have a boy, no matter what! She was steadfast in her faith. Together with her husband, she even got the baby's room painted blue to further declare their faith that they were having a boy. Delivery time came, they went into hospital, and lo and behold, when the baby came out, it was a boy! This is a real story. This story should encourage someone to step out in faith. Have faith, and let your faith be with works that support what you are believing for! Be *crazy* in what you are believing God for! Don't you *ever* give room to doubt and sabotage your own answer!

Sow a Seed: Sow a seed to back up your faith for whatever you are believing God for. Sowing a seed can be in the form of giving money, working in the house of God, or doing something for someone voluntarily to meet that person's needs. There are many ways you can sow a seed as a way of presenting your works before God: Sometimes God by His Spirit can reveal to you what steps you ought to take in order to get your breakthrough. Sowing a seed by revelation is always effective, especially if you follow instinct by obeying the Holy Spirit.

I remember one time when I wanted to buy a car. I desperately needed a breakthrough and God's hand and guidance. There was a group of construction workers working on my father's property for an entire week. On the last day of their job, I got prompted to wake up at 4 a.m. and prepare a meal for the workers that would last them through the whole day. I did as my instincts led me to and prepared the meal for the next three hours. And then, after I had finished preparing the meal, I went before God and presented my works before Him, asking for a blessing in securing the car. And to tell you the truth, God's favour was upon me, and I got more than I had bargained for that very same day! My breakthrough was instant! Always make it a habit to present your works before God and receive your blessing. Create a reason for God to bless you, and present the reason before Him in prayer. There are so many examples of my personal life that I could give, but I'll stop here.

Purpose in your heart to have faith and to believe!

Principle #7:

THE HEALTH FACTOR

Take good care of your body, being unhealthy costs! You are what you eat.
—David Conellias

First things first: Get your thoughts healthy first, because no matter how healthy you eat, and how much you exercise, if your thoughts are not in order, neither will your body be. Your overall well-being is dependent on your thought life. When you fear catching a certain illness or condition just because someone in your family had it, chances are you will get it. Remember, you attract what you harbour in the confines of your soul.

Eat Healthy

Many of us are well aware of this principle, and yet a lot ignore it. I've often heard people say that the reason they don't like healthy food is because "some of it doesn't taste good" or "it's expensive". It's sometimes hard to convince people with such a mentality to adopt healthy eating habits. Yes, some of the foods are expensive, but years down the line, your unhealthy eating habits may cost you more than better food would have. Everything works in a process. You might not see the effects of your bad eating habits now, but years down the line, everything will catch up with you, especially if you continue down the wrong road. And yes, some of it tastes bad, but the more you force yourself to eat it, the more you develop a taste for it, and the more your body will thank you. I like what one man said: "You are free to eat whatever you want, your diet will not keep you from heaven, but if you continually eat unhealthy foods, you will get there much sooner."

Living Foods

We should eat more of *living foods* as opposed to *dead foods*. God put everything we need into nature. According to Genesis, God gave us every "herb that yield seeds" and "every tree which yields seeds" for food and medicine. He put everything we would need into the soil, so that the herbs and trees could absorb the vital nutrients that we would need. That's why you find that every fruit and vegetable contains different vitamins and nutrients that are necessary for our health. The food in the Garden of Eden was *fresh* food straight from the source, and never microwaved or cooked, either. All Adam and Eve did was to pluck fruits from trees and herbs that were made available to them. That's why you also find that fruits and vegetables are most nutritious in their natural, uncooked state. Hence the term *living foods*, because the general composition of nutrients and minerals hasn't been altered or destroyed through cooking (conventional or microwave heat).

Living foods include fresh organic fruits and vegetables, whole grains, and good fats (monounsaturated fats as well as omega-3 fats found in foods such as coldwater fish, flaxseed, walnuts, olive oil, and macadamia nuts). Not all fats are bad; your body needs these good fats for healthy heart and brain function. Avoid frying in polyunsaturated fats such as sunflower oil, soybean oil, corn oil, and vegetable oil. Frying at high temperatures converts these oils to dangerous lipid peroxides which create tremendous amounts of free radicals. And free radicals are not good for you either; they lead to cancer and make you age quicker, as well as damaging your liver. Most of these oils have been processed under heat and have most nutrients removed from them.

Meat is to be eaten with caution and in moderation. Now I will let you do most of the research on your own, because this is quite a broad topic and I'm just summarising what I've come to learn myself.

Why Organic:

Organic food is food that is grown without the use of artificial pesticides and chemical fertilisers. Organic foods are grown, or produced with the addition of only animal or vegetable fertilisers to the soil, such as manure, bone meal, and compost. They deliver superior nutrition without the harmful chemicals or foreign substances that can be harmful to our bodies/health.

Dead Foods

Dead foods include all processed meat and in fact anything processed. These are usually found in most fast foods and tinned foods; sugar (and we all know that too much of that leads to diabetes, osteoporosis, accelerated ageing, elevated cholesterol, aggravated yeast problems, an impaired immune system, behavioural disorders, and obesity); and white flour. I was shocked when I found out that the natural colour of flour before being processed is grey, but because no one wants to eat grey bread, the flour is then bleached so that it becomes white! (I can see many people gasping; I reacted the same way.)

All of this made me see why God gave the Children of Israel a diet to follow in Leviticus; it was for their own benefit. No wonder there was none feeble (lacking physical strength, especially as a result of age or illness) among all the 3.5 million Jews who travelled in the wilderness! Their bodies were strong and healthy and disease-resistant. The Lord gave Moses instructions on what to eat and what to avoid in Leviticus 11 and Deuteronomy 14, and guess what? These rules had and still have a scientific basis for good health. Now don't pull the "God takes care of my body and health" card on me! Yes, He takes care of us, but He gives the wisdom on how to maintain that health. The choice is ours. It's not forced on us, and it's only for the willing. God will still love you even to your deathbed. Be wise, get wisdom, and get understanding!

Examples of healthy foods and what they do for our bodies:

- **Extra-virgin olive oil:** Contains vitamin E, oleocanthal, and antioxidant compounds, which can reduce inflammation. This oil is commonly used in the Mediterranean diet. It's high in monounsaturated fats and can help lower cholesterol. Cutting the amount of saturated fats and incorporating more of monounsaturated and polyunsaturated fats can decrease your risk of heart disease, and using extra virgin olive oil is a perfect way of doing this.
- **Almonds:** A rich source of protein, high in calcium and monounsaturated fats (heart-healthy oils like olive oil). When consumed regularly, they can help lower your bad LDL cholesterol and risk of heart disease.
- **Walnuts:** Though nuts are high in calories and fat, the monounsaturated fat in nuts is healthier than the saturated fat in meat and dairy products. Walnuts are high in omega-3 fatty acid, which is good for the heart, and carry some of the highest antioxidant content among all nuts.
- **Chia seeds:** A god source of plant omega-3 fatty acid; protects against inflammation, arthritis and heart disease.
- **Flax seeds:** Just like chia seeds, they are high in omega-3 fatty acid, called ALA, and very good for the heart. Grind them before you eat them though.
- **Lentils:** Full of iron, fibre, and protein.
- **Kidney beans:** Good source of magnesium and potassium. Their fibre content helps reduce bad LDL cholesterol, fighting off heart disease. They help keep blood pressure in check. They are also a good source of protein and iron, making them a great meat substitute for vegetarians. They contain disease-fighting antioxidants.
- **Legumes:** High in protein, packed with fibre, high in the powerful phytochemical anthocyanin (also found in blueberries); these are antioxidants that help fight disease.

- **Blueberries:** Good source of vitamins C and E. Their deep vibrant colours mean that they are high in antioxidant compounds; these are compounds that help fight free radicals in our bodies, thus preventing disease. Blueberries are high in the heart-protective carotenoids and flavonoids, and they aid heart, memory and urinary tract health.
- **Apples:** High in fibre, especially pectin fibre, which targets and clears away LDL (the bad cholesterol). The beneficial compounds are mainly found in the skin and include high levels of phytochemicals, which have antioxidant and anti-inflammatory properties.
- **Oatmeal:** High in beta-glucan, a fibre that lowers LDL cholesterol. Steel-cut oats are the best, because they contain no additives and are minimally processed. Ideal as a post-workout food since it contains energy-producing B vitamins and carbohydrates that replenish your muscles.
- **Whole-wheat bread:** At least half the grains you eat must whole; these include the bran, germ and endosperm. Refined grains (used in white bread and white rice), are milled, meaning bran and germ have been removed to give the grains a soft, finer texture. This process strips the grains of dietary fibre, iron and several B vitamins. Whole grains are good for your heart, help lower cholesterol, help tackle obesity, and help regulate blood sugar and blood pressure. Go for 100 per cent wholegrain.
- **Red wine:** This is not a licence to drink excessively, but, yes, a glass of this stuff can do good to your body. It contains a compound called resveratrol, which has been linked to longevity and lowers risks of diabetes and heart disease.
- **Dark chocolate:** A good way to treat yourself if you are a chocolate lover. It is better than milk chocolate because of its high concentration of cocoa, which is packed with disease-fighting antioxidant plant chemicals called flavonol. Those antioxidants can help reduce the risk of blood clots and lower blood pressure and inflammation as well as improve insulin resistance.

- **Tuna:** High in protein, selenium, vitamin B, and omega-3 fatty acids.
- **Salmon:** Rich in vitamin D and omega-3 fatty acids, which protect your heart as well.
- **Meat:** High in protein, vitamin E, vitamin B, iron, zinc, and magnesium. But it is important to differentiate between lean meats and those high in saturated fats and cholesterol. Boneless, skinless chicken breasts and turkey cutlets are your leanest poultry choices; as for beef, round steaks and roasts, top loin, top sirloin, chuck shoulder, and arm roasts are the leanest cuts.
- **Tomatoes:** Contain a long list of nutrients, including vitamins A, C, and K. Also contains the antioxidant lycopene, which helps lower inflammation and cholesterol, and again is good for your heart health.
- **Brussels sprouts:** Contain glucosinolates, which are sulphur compounds that help lower risks of prostate, lung, stomach, and breast cancers.
- **Eggplant:** Packed with fibre; contains the whole gamut of B vitamins, which give you all the energy you need. Also contains powerful antioxidants that protect brain cells and control lipid levels.
- **Sweet potato:** Not only are they sweet but they are packed with high levels of potassium that help lower blood pressure and reduce stroke risk. The skin is packed with fibre, too.
- **Spinach:** Packed with nutrients, including iron, calcium, and vitamin A, which keeps the eyes and skin healthy. Spinach also packs folate, which helps the body form healthy red blood cells and prevents birth defects during pregnancy.
- **Bananas:** High in potassium, which aids blood pressure and is critical for the proper function of the muscular and digestive systems.
- **Avocados:** Contains carotene antioxidants (lycopene and beta-carotene). Best way to eat avocadoes is to peel them, because the greatest concentration of carotenoids in avocados lies in the dark green flesh that lies just beneath the skin. This

vegetable contains anti-inflammatory properties, which are found in the fat contained within it (phytosterols, oleic acid and polyhrdroxylated fatty alcohols). Even though high in fat, the fat is actually good for our heart and overall health. It can help relieve osteoarthritis and rheumatoid arthritis, promote blood sugar regulation, and help prevent cancer in the mouth, skin and prostate gland.

- **Lemons:** Have a glass of warm lemon water every morning 30 minutes before eating anything, to give the Lemon time to enter your blood stream and do its job. Lemon is rich in vitamin C, calcium, potassium and pectin fibre, helps the liver detoxify thus purifying the blood, rejuvenates the skin from within and brings a glow to your face, prevents the formation of wrinkles and acne, paves the way for losing weight faster, boosts the immune system (a good remedy for colds and viruses), and balances the pH levels in the body (lemon is acidic, but when consumed into our bodies, it turns alkaline). It aids digestion and encourages the production of bile. It helps reduce pain and inflammation in joints and knees as it dissolves uric acid. Potassium content helps nourish brain and nerve cells. Lemon also helps maintain eye health. Take that lemon, and don't mix it with anything else except water.

The list is endless: We have broccoli; beet root; oranges, which are a good source of vitamin C protecting vision and skin; pumpkins containing vitamin A and beta carotene; strawberries, good for fighting cancer and ageing; cherries, which help calm your nervous system; grapes, which help relax blood vessels; pineapples, which help fight arthritis; kiwis, which increase bone mass; watermelons, which help control the heart rate; and mangos, which help prevent cancer. I could go on and on, but the rest is up to you to research on your own.

Spices and Herbs

Spices and herbs not only add flavour to our favourite dishes but also contain a myriad of health benefits. I'm going to list just a few for your benefit.

- **Cinnamon:** There is four types of cinnamon: Ceylon, Korintje, Saigon, and Cassia (cheap and commonly used). The best is Ceylon (true) cinnamon. It can lower blood sugar, triglycerides, LDL, and total cholesterol in people with type 2 diabetes. Half a teaspoon a day is enough. Too much is not advised because cinnamon can have thinning effect on the blood.
- **Cumin:** May help people with diabetes keep blood sugar levels in check. It has powerful germ-fighting properties that might prevent stomach ulcers. A very good source of calcium, iron, and magnesium.
- **Ginseng:** Decreases blood sugar levels in people with type 2 diabetes, slows colorectal cancer cell growth, helps fight colds, and boosts immunity.
- **Turmeric:** Main spice in curry. Contains curcumin, which can inhibit the growth of cancer cells. It is used to treat everything from depression to liver disease to skin ailments. It has helped people with arthritis and with heartburn.
- **Rosemary:** Stops gene mutations that could lead to cancer and may help prevent damage to blood vessels that raises heart attack risk. Might also stimulate the production of acetylcholine, which in turn helps boost learning and memory.
- **Garlic:** Destroys cancer cells and may disrupt the metabolism of tumour cells. It also helps boost immune system and has antibacterial properties.
- **Paprika:** Contains capsaicin, whose anti-inflammatory and antioxidant effects may lower the risk of cancer (also found in cayenne and red chilli peppers).
- **Ginger:** Can decrease motion sickness and nausea; may relieve pain and swelling associated with arthritis. Ginger can also

hinder blood clotting and has got anti-inflammatory properties (works wonders for singers with swollen vocal chords).

- **Anise:** Can help calm an upset stomach and help with coughs and runny noses. Because of presumed oestrogen-like properties, anise may increase milk flow in breastfeeding mothers, treat menstrual symptoms, and boost libido. It's also a good source of fibre, calcium, and iron, among other nutrients.
- **Lavender:** Has got calming and soothing effects, which help ease stress and promote sleep. Having lavender part of a spice mix can help beat bloating. Its antioxidants, known as polyphenols in oil form, can stop itching and swelling when applied to the skin.
- **Mint:** Helpful in treating a number of digestive ailments, most notably irritable bowel syndrome.
- **Nutmeg:** A good solution for stomach problems; seems to fight off bacteria and fungi. A solid source of fibre with anti-inflammatory properties, which could help smooth blemishes when applied directly onto skin.
- **Oregano:** Possesses both antibacterial and antifungal properties that make it effective against some forms of food-borne illnesses and even some antibiotic- resistant infections. Also effective against yeast-based infections.
- **Thyme:** Bursting with antioxidants, like thymol, flavonoids, apigenin, naringenin, luteolin, and thymonin. Antioxidants prevent cellular damage that can boost overall health and help prevent cancer, inflammation, signs of ageing, and more.
- **Nettle:** Usually taken as a tea. Nettle can help stimulate lymph system to boost immunity, relieves arthritis, promotes release of uric acid from joints, helps relieve menstrual cramps and bloating, helps break down kidney stones, reduces hypertension, reduces inflammation, reduces the risk of prostate cancer, minimises skin problems, helps with osteoarthritis, reduces gingivitis and prevents plaque when used as a mouth wash, destroys intestinal worms and parasites, supports endocrine

health by helping the thyroid, spleen, and pancreas. This herb works many wonders!

Gardening and Farming

If you have the land and space, invest in your own garden of fruits and vegetables. Invest in a greenhouse. A little hobby in gardening or farming will not kill you. It is actually refreshing. Invest in an orchard if you can. Find out what fruits grow best in your area. It is worth the try and investment. At least you will enjoy freshly grown and organic produce from your own hands. Trust me, you will get the satisfaction out of it. God was the Master Farmer in the Garden of Eden, and we should learn from our Father. Besides, His DNA is already in us. All we have to do is a little bit of research and get working.

In a Nutshell: A Balanced Diet

Keeping a balanced diet is paramount. A balanced diet consists of certain ingredients for effective nutrition. With the right foods, a better quality of life will be sustained. If you want, you can have a balanced diet plan that you can follow through every day. There are types of fruit and vegetables that should be included with every meal. Do your heart, brain, hormones, nerves, and cells a favour by consuming the right *good* fats.

Protein: When derived from food, protein is broken down into amino acids. These twenty or so amino acids are building blocks for the body to naturally create protein. Apart from providing us with energy, protein is essential in tissue, cell, and organ health. Lack of protein leads to reduction in muscle mass and weakened immunity, heart, and respiratory systems. It can also lead to hair loss, and severe deficiency can lead to diseases such as kwashiorkor. Lack of protein also slows down growth rate. Proteins can be derived from eggs (preferably raw), fish, meat, poultry, cheese, milk, and beans. For those undertaking a rigorous workout routine, a protein diet proves beneficial. It provides you with the energy you need for endurance during long and intense workout sessions. Protein helps repair damaged muscle and aids in the body's natural healing process.

Carbohydrates: Carbohydrates are essential for a balanced diet, especially complex carbohydrates. Avoid simple carbohydrates like white flour and rice, which may lead to obesity-related diseases. Complex carbohydrates include items such as whole grains, beans, vegetables, and some fruits; these are suggested as part of a balanced diet.

Good fats: Polyunsaturated and monounsaturated fats are essential to a healthy diet. They benefit the heart, brain, nerves, hormones, and cells. These fats are also good for skin, hair, and nails. Examples of monounsaturated fats include peanut, canola, and olive oil. Polyunsaturated fats include omega-3 and omega-6 fatty acids, which the body cannot produce. These fats help reduce the risk of cardiovascular disease, prevent dementia and remedy depression. Sources include fish, walnuts as well as sunflower, soybean and flaxseed oil.

Fruits and vegetable: These are a *must* for a balanced diet. Your menu should include dark leafy green vegetables**,** which are packed with amazing nutrients, such as calcium, potassium, zinc, magnesium, iron as well as and vitamin A, C, E, and K. Other types of vegetables and fruit should be added, too. Fruits add a natural sweetness to your diet, along with fibre, vitamins, and antioxidants.

Dairy and other vitamin D and calcium products: These are necessary nutrients for healthy bones. Calcium is absorbed in the small intestine from the vitamin D content of dairy products. Dairy includes milk and cheese. Calcium is also found in collard greens, dark leafy vegetables, legumes, and dried beans

Cook healthy, too. Avoid microwaves if possible, because a study in *Science News* in 1998 found that just six minutes of microwaved cooking destroyed half the vitamin B_{12} in dairy foods and meat, a much higher rate of destruction than other cooking techniques. Heat in general alters nutrient content in foods and destroys most of the vitamins. Cook wisely. Don't overcook your vegetables; they are better steamed.

Tip: Avoid eating a heavy meal just before you go to bed, especially after 8 p.m., and two hours before you sleep, it adds extra pounds to your waist. If you are trying to lose weight, this is a tip to consider.

Fasting: Believe it or not, fasting is actually good for you! It helps detoxify your body, repair cells, tissues, and organs, at the same time eliminating foreign toxins and natural metabolic waste. Your kidneys will thank you. When you fast, you rest the digestive system, promote greater mental clarity, increase energy levels, promote an inner stillness, and enhance spiritual connection. Your prayer time is enhanced because you focus more on the inner man. It gives you a sense of achieving and conquering. Don't be surprised when you receive constructive ideas during fasting. Fasting initiates the body's own healing mechanisms; it is the greatest remedy to the physician within. Sixty-five per cent of the body's energy is directed to the digestive organs after a heavy meal (that's why you feel sleepy). Free up this energy by fasting, and it can be diverted to healing and recuperation. You feel emotionally calm, clearer, and happier. Fasting can help cope with depression and help improve concentration. You experience less anxiety, sleep better, and wake up more refreshed.

Breakfast: It matters how well you start your day. Kick-start your day by eating a healthy and wholesome breakfast to boost your metabolism and immune system. Breakfast is the most important meal of the day because it sets a lot of things in our bodies in positive motion. A homemade smoothie first thing in the morning is a good way to kick-start you for the day. Smoothies are easy to make at home. You can spark a little bit of invention and come up with your own recipes.

Dieting: Personally, I don't diet; I just eat healthy and keep fit. If you want to lose weight, starving yourself is not the best option. Instead eat small portions of food throughout the day whilst maintaining a balanced diet. Don't eat three big heavy meals per day either; it's not good for your metabolism. Rather spread out your meals proportionately throughout the day. Drink enough water and exercise. Avoid excessive consumption of takeaway foods; learn to eat fresh, healthy home-cooked meals. If takeaway cannot be avoided, go for the healthiest option.

Remember to also eat your portion of five fruits or vegetables a day; exceeding that is not illegal either. And also keep a balanced diet every day.

Eating out: I love the Mediterranean diet. When I go out, my first choice of restaurant is Greek or Italian. The rest is according to discretion.

Sodium chloride: Many of us are consuming too much salt. Most of the foods we eat already contain 75 per cent of recommended daily intake of salt. These foods include bread, breakfast cereals, and ready meals. Too much salt causes a rise in blood pressure. High blood pressure has no symptoms and can develop into heart disease or stroke. Cutting down on salt lowers blood pressure. High-salt foods include anchovies, bacon, gravy granules, cheese, olives, pickles, prawns, salami, salt fish, soy sauce, stock cubes, and yeast extract. Also watch out for other foods like bread products, pasta sauces, crisps, take-away meals, soup, sandwiches, sausages, and condiments in general. Once again, the key here is moderation.

For your cooking, try and use sea salt. It's healthier than iodized salt but doesn't lower your sodium levels at all. Salt is salt. Sea salt, however, can strengthen the immune system, is alkalising to the body (your body functions well under alkaline conditions, as compared to acidic conditions), and can help in weight loss. A bath in it helps relieve dry and itchy skin and other serious skin conditions (it improves circulation in the skin and hydrates tissues so that skin heals). It helps people with asthmatic conditions and is good for heart health, diabetes, osteoporosis, and muscle spasms (because of small amounts of potassium found in it).

Alcohol: Too much beer gives you a pot belly and is generally not good for your body. You basically overload your liver with toxins, which in turn might eventually give you liver sclerosis.

Smoking: Everybody knows that smoking kills. Smoking makes you age faster and leaves nicotine deposits on your teeth (yellow substance). It's not good for your respiratory system and can eventually lead to lung cancer. Think about it! Be wary of passive smoke too.

Skin Health

Esther 2:12

Amplified Bible (AMP)

Now when the turn of each maiden came to go in to King Ahasuerus, after the regulations for the women had been carried out for twelve months—since this was the regular period for their beauty treatments, six months with oil of myrrh and six months with sweet spices and perfumes and the things for the purifying of the women—

I used to wonder how people in ancient times looked after their skin, and I got the answer from that portion of Scripture taken from the book of Esther. Obviously I did a bit of further research to be sure I was right. They didn't have the modern-day skin moisturizers, which are composed of different petrochemicals, parabens, and other ingredients which might be harsh to the skin, but they had natural oils. The most common oil used especially in the Mediterranean region was olive oil. They used it both for cooking and as an effective skin moisturiser. When I discovered the significant benefits of using some of these natural oils as part of my daily skincare regime, I began to use fewer and fewer chemicals on my skin, because the natural stuff works ten times better for me. Now, I'm not saying everyone should revert to using natural oils, but you could keep an open mind and try them out.

It is important to look after your skin by applying appropriate moisturisers (besides water, which moisturises our skin from within) to help protect the epidermal layer from harsh weather conditions and other factors that might affect skin health. The list of oils below is just a suggestion; everybody has got different remedies and methods that work well for them. The important thing is to know what works well for your skin type and to stick to that. The good thing about these oils is that they are *natural*; make sure they are 100 per cent natural before you buy any particular one. For instance, if you are buying *argan oil*, the name *argan* should be the only ingredient on the label, and it should read something like this: 100 per cent ARGAN OIL, or just ARGAN OIL with nothing else following. You can always ask at the counter before you buy, just to be sure.

As for those with oily skin, you might be thinking, *Why add more oil to my skin?* You are not the only one who thought that. But I discovered that avoidance of these natural oils actually impairs my skin's ability to heal. The right combination of oils for your skincare needs provides powerful properties to normalise oil production, reduce signs of ageing, and refine skin texture. When you use the right natural oils for your skin type, they do not cause oily skin or clog pores. It is only when we use synthetic oils (like mineral oil) or heavy (comedogenic) oils do we run into these problems. Using plant oils as carriers and blending them with therapeutic oils creates moisturisers that effectively nourish and balance your skin by delivering the most potent form of nutrients directly onto your skin. The key here is moderation. Some of these oils can be harsh if not used or mixed correctly. For example, when you look at tea tree oil, as much as it is good for fighting spots and blemishes, too much of it can make your skin irritated (red or flaky). So use sparingly, but be consistent. Similarly, straight clove essential oil will burn your skin. Always use the right combination, and ask if you are not sure. Do your research well.

Carrier Oils

Also known as vegetable oil or base oil, carrier oils are used to dilute essential oils before applying them to the skin in massage or aromatherapy. They carry the essential oil onto the skin. Unlike essential oils, they do not contain a concentrated aroma, though some might have a distinct smell. Neither do they evaporate like essential oils, which are more volatile. The carrier oils should be as natural and unadulterated as possible, preferably cold-pressed or macerated. The good thing is, most of them don't necessarily have to be mixed with essential oils to be used on a daily basis as part of a skincare regime. Usually you can apply them directly onto the skin as they are, but always check first.

Examples of carrier oils include the following: olive oil, grape seed oil, sweet almond oil, apricot oil, sesame oil, evening primrose, rapeseed oil, sunflower oil, jojoba oil, emu oil, castor oil, walnut oil, peanut oil, pecan oil, macadamia oil, coconut oil, hazelnut oil, and cocoa butter. (If you are allergic to nuts, please stay away from the nut-based oils.)

Essential Oils

An essential oil is a concentrated hydrophobic liquid containing volatile aroma compounds from plants. Essential oils carry the distinctive scent, or essence, of the plant they are extracted from. Essential oils are usually "oil loving" (lipophilic) compounds that are not miscible with water. Most of them need to be mixed with a base oil to avoid skin irritation, but some of them can be applied directly on the skin with no adverse effects. It is worth finding out which ones. When it comes to mixing, a common ratio of essential oil dispersed in a carrier oil is 0.5 to 3 per cent (most under 10 per cent), depending on its purpose. Some essential oils – especially the citrus peel oils – increase the skin's vulnerability to sunlight. As I said before, research and find out what works perfectly for your skin type.

Examples of essential oils include the following: myrrh, frankincense, bergamot, ylang-ylang, clove, chamomile, hyssop, eucalyptus, oregano, peppermint, rosemary, patchouli, tea tree, juniper, nutmeg, and valerian. (I've named just a few, but there are loads more.)

Oils You Can Safely Use on a Daily Basis

Olive oil: Look for the term "first cold press" on the bottle. This means that the oil hasn't been exposed to high temperatures that can alter or destroy its antioxidant properties. Olive oil is mostly recommended for people with very dry skin. It is moisturising and full of nutrients and fatty acids; it *may* even protect against skin cancer. This oil is safe to apply directly onto bare skin.

Argan oil: Known for its anti-aging properties, argan oil contains high levels of Vitamin E and anti-inflammatory fatty acids. Argan oil's antioxidants won't break down in sunlight, making it a good choice to wear during the day. Though very pricey in its original state, argan oil can help fight dry and flaky skin, and even acne. The oil itself *should* be very expensive, in fact; if it's too cheap, I would question its authenticity. It is safe to apply directly onto bare skin.

Grapeseed oil: This oil comes from the seeds of pressed grapes, and it's high in antioxidants. It is beneficial for skin types from dry and flaky to greasy. Grapeseed oil helps regulate the body's natural oil production. It can be applied directly onto the skin to even out skin tone and prevent signs of ageing. And the good news is, it's inexpensive.

Carrot seed oil: Carrots are generally high in antioxidants, especially the powerful cancer-fighting beta-carotene. The same is true for the seeds of the wild carrot plant, which are pressed to create this common skincare ingredient. The oil may help reduce inflammation in dry, irritated skin and can even help fight off precancerous skin lesions on skin exposed to too much sun. That's why you find that carrot-seed oil is often added to sunscreen and other anti-aging creams and serums.

Peppermint oil: The naturally astringent properties of this oil help clear out clogged pores and control the skin's natural oil production. This is why you might feel a slight tingling and warmth on your skin when you apply this oil or any product that contains peppermint oil. Like all other essential oils, it is very potent by itself, and it can irritate the skin if applied directly. Instead, add a few drops to a carrier oil like olive or sweet almond oil, or even place a few drops in your bath or look for commercial products that contain the blend.

Jojoba oil: Made from pressed jojoba seeds, this oil's composition is the closest thing in nature to our own sebum. It creates a quickly absorbing, lightweight moisturiser for all skin types and penetrates deep into the skin. If you struggle with oily skin, a jojoba blend is the way to go, because it will dissolve excess sebum and allow the pores to breathe. I remember recommending this to a friend with oily skin, and they felt the results instantly. Again, jojoba oil can be applied directly onto bare skin.

Moringa oil: *Moringa Oleifera* in Latin; used by ancient Egyptians as early as 2000 BC. This oil contains an *extraordinarily* high amount of antioxidants, and as we already know, these antioxidants help fight against ageing and protect the skin from sun damage. The antioxidant content and fatty acid profile can diminish the appearance of wrinkles, lighten skin tone, and deeply moisturise the skin. Again, it is safe to apply directly onto skin.

Rosehip oil: Offers superb hydrating properties. This oil instantly revives your skin with a deep penetrating level of moisture. Good for those whose skin faces environmental stressors, such as dry air and wind. Rosehip can restore the ideal balance of moisture to stressed skin. The oil provides anti-aging properties and has been known for its regeneration properties and for scar reduction.

Tamanu oil: This is one of my favourite oils. It's extremely soothing and offers relief from eczema, rashes, sunburn, skin irritation and inflammation. It helps restore and regenerate skin tissue. It contains antimicrobial and antioxidant properties, thus making it an alternative treatment for breakouts. Safe to use directly on skin. You don't need to use a lot; just a little drop can go a long way.

That's about it on skin health. Some of these oils (if not all) like argan, castor, jojoba, and olive oil are also good for your hair. They help keep hair moisturised and add lustre to it. Avoid using synthetic oils and comedogenic oils, because these can clog your hair follicles and interfere with hair growth. Even when washing your hair, avoid using harsh chemicals which strip your natural oils away. Try and use the best combination of natural products that help maintain and replace natural nutrients that your hair needs. Washing your hair now and again helps unclog hair follicles by removing excess dirt and oil, thereby making way for healthy hair growth.

Drink That Water! Cut the Coffee and Soft Drink

Our bodies are about 70 to 80 per cent water. Isn't it intriguing that even a growing foetus is completely surrounded by amniotic fluid (waters) for protection and nourishment? Now that should say a lot about the importance of water in our bodies, and why we need to stay adequately hydrated.

- ❖ Muscles consist of 75 per cent water
- ❖ The brain consists of 95 per cent water
- ❖ Bones consists of 25 per cent water
- ❖ Blood consists of 83 per cent water

It is recommended we take in at least 2 l of water per day to replace lost fluid due to perspiration, breathing, urination, exercise, and so forth. Water (not juice, fizzy pops, or coffee) is a vital element of our health. Going for long periods without water could prove detrimental to your health and overall well-being. Heavy coffee drinkers should seriously consider cutting back. Otherwise they might have to drink more water than normal to replace lost fluid because of the drug caffeine. For now, let me show you the functions of water in our body.

Functions of water in the body:

- ❖ Protects and moisturises joints
- ❖ Moisturises the air in lungs
- ❖ Transports oxygen and nutrients into body cells
- ❖ Helps with metabolism
- ❖ Helps with digestion
- ❖ Regulates body temperature
- ❖ Protects vital organs
- ❖ Helps organs absorb nutrients better
- ❖ Detoxifies

Now, that in itself should explain a lot! Most people are dehydrated, and as a result their health suffers. Coffee and soft drinks are not to be counted as part of your water intake. Actually coffee is a diuretic because of the drug caffeine found in the coffee bean and most soft beverages. Yes, caffeine does stimulate the central nervous system and metabolism, but it also flushes water out of your system, thus creating an imbalance of water in your body. It elevates heart rate and muscle twitching and can cause insomnia. As for soft drinks, they have got a high sugar content and some contain caffeine as well. They will basically "help" you gain extra weight if that's what you are looking for. Let me list the benefits of drinking water, and the causes of dehydration on your health:

Benefits

- ❖ You will look younger and your skin will be healthier, because water helps replenish skin tissues, moisturise the skin, and increase skin elasticity.
- ❖ Water helps with digestion and constipation. Fibre and water go hand in hand so that you can have your daily bowel movement.

❖ Water relieves fatigue: It is used by the body to flush out toxins and waste products. If your body is water deprived, your heart, for example, needs to work much harder to pump out the oxygenated blood to all cells. So are the rest of the vital organs; your organs will be exhausted and so will you.

❖ Reduce the risk of cancer: Drinking water can help reduce bladder and colon cancer. Water dilutes the concentration of cancer-causing agents in the urine and shortens the time in which they are in contact with the bladder lining.

❖ Feel healthier: Water helps fight against flu and other ailments, like kidney stones and heart attack. Water can improve your immune system. Mixed with lemon, it can help combat respiratory disease, intestinal problems, rheumatism, and arthritis.

❖ Exercise better: Water helps regulate body temperature. That means more energy when exercising and more fuel to the muscles.

❖ Water helps relieve headaches and back pains caused by dehydration.

❖ Water helps you lose weight, because it flashes down the by-products of fat breakdown. It also helps reduce hunger, and it's an effective appetite suppressant, so you'll eat less. The good thing is that water contains zero calories.

❖ Water can actually help you combat acid reflux by diluting excess hydrochloric acid in the stomach. Most dehydrated people suffer from heart burn.

Effects of dehydration:

❖ Tiredness, migraine, acid reflux, muscle cramps, kidney problems, constipation, irregular blood pressure, dry skin, and in severe cases death.

Dehydration symptoms:

- ❖ Dark urine (dark yellow or orange in colour): The darker the urine, the more dehydrated you are. The urine is dark because of concentration of undiluted toxins. Normal urine should be pale yellow when someone is properly hydrated. If it's colourless like water, chances are you are over-hydrated. Please note, some medication can cause urine to be dark yellow as well.
- ❖ Fatigue: Water is an energy source, and it boosts your energy.
- ❖ Thirst: This is the most obvious sign of dehydration. Don't wait until you are thirsty to drink water; drink it regularly.
- ❖ Dry skin: This is the largest body organ, and it requires its fair share of water.
- ❖ Hunger: Most people mistake hunger for indication to eat more when actually their body is crying out for more water. So before you eat, grab a glass of water first.

When getting bottled water, make sure it's got a pH above 7.2 (alkaline state). Alkalinity and acidity are measured in terms of pH. On the pH scale of 1 to 14, 7.0 is considered neutral. Anything under 7.0 is acidic; anything over 7.0 is alkaline. Blood has a constant pH of 7.4, which means it's alkaline. When your body is acidic, it is less efficient at removing toxins. Many health problems are associated with being too acidic, including fibromyalgia, chronic fatigue, arteriosclerosis, most cancers, arthritis, diabetes, autoimmune disease, osteoporosis, and most degenerative diseases. By consuming adequate amounts of alkaline water and foods, you can increase your urine pH from 7.0 to 7.5, also bringing your tissues back to alkaline state. You can create alkaline water from tap water or spring water by using alkalizing filters. Ask your general practitioner for a body pH test, or go to your local pharmacy or drug store and ask how you can do it yourself.

Drink your water thirty minutes before meals, or two hours after. You don't want it to interfere with food absorption.

Exercise

Most people hate this word, because it involves commitment and putting in some effort. If you have a certain degree of laziness in you, you will struggle with his point. Having a busy schedule is not an excuse; you should learn time management! Exercise doesn't have to be vigorous and strenuous like some think. It can be a simple 30-minute walk in the park. Instead of driving into the town centre, why not walk there instead if town is within a reasonable distance? Instead of taking the elevator, why not take the stairs? If you want to go the extra mile, join a gym membership and get sweating. What most people don't know is that sweating is actually good for your health. It is the body's way of cooling down of course, and more importantly, toxins are excreted from your body through sweating. This is all achieved when you exercise; it is a good form of detoxing. Avoid vigorous exercise at least 3 hours before going to bed; otherwise you'll have trouble sleeping at night.

Fact: We get 90 per cent of vitamin D through the sun (ten to fifteen minutes in the sun is what most people need). Vitamin D is needed for bone growth, cell growth, inflammation reduction, as well as neuromuscular and immune function. A twenty-minute walk in the park or outside can prove beneficial. It can help you cope with stress, lose weight, spur creativity, improve concentration, and boost energy. We respond well to nature. I'm not surprised, because when God created man, he placed them in a garden with trees, plants, and herbs – nature in general, and not in a house! Don't be stuck indoors all the times. Get out and get some fresh air. Our first habitation was a garden. That should explain why we are naturally drawn to nature. Gardening can even help dementia and stroke patients improve social skills and confidence while increasing dexterity and mobility. Nature helps us relax by helping decrease stress levels. Nature helps shift towards more positive moods.

A liken someone who doesn't exercise to an abandoned pond. Wherever there's stagnant water, there is a lot of algae build up. All sorts of insects come to breed in such water. The water becomes stale and polluted and in most cases releases a pungent smell because of inactivity. Similarly to us humans, the less we exercise, the more our body becomes like the stagnant pond. It will attract all sorts of disease, there's a lot of toxin build-up in the blood, and most of it stores up as fat (and then you gain weight). Your metabolism becomes sluggish, you feel tired most of the times, and to top it up, your heart suffers in most cases. The more fat builds up (bad cholesterol) around your waist, the more likely your heart suffers. And there is no excuse for the skinny person, because you can still build up bad cholesterol in your blood and around your heart and suffer in the end. The greatest threat to health is inactivity. Have an exercise regime that you faithfully follow. Be faithful to your own body!

Benefits of exercise:

- ❖ Exercise promotes weight loss and controls it. Thirty minutes of energetic exercise three to four times a week can prove beneficial.
- ❖ Exercise is good for your heart; helps reduce LDL cholesterol, the kind that clogs arteries; reduces blood pressure; improves insulin sensitivity; improves heart muscle function; and diminishes chances of developing blood clots.
- ❖ Exercise lowers high blood pressure.
- ❖ Exercise is an excellent de-stressor. It tackles stress and depression, thus enhancing your mood.
- ❖ Exercise prevents colds. The more you sweat, the more your body flushes out toxins, bacteria, and viruses.
- ❖ Exercise reduces severity of asthma (swimming is best for asthmatics).
- ❖ Exercise reduces diabetic complications.
- ❖ Exercise prevents osteoporosis.
- ❖ Exercise promotes a healthy pregnancy.
- ❖ Exercise promotes brain health
- ❖ Exercise has anti-ageing effects. It enhances blood flow to the brain, possibly reducing risk of stroke. It improves reasoning and memory. It arouses the brain and slows down degeneration of the central nervous system.

❖ Exercise plays a role in cancer prevention.

❖ Exercise improves sleeping patterns, especially relaxation exercises (they help ease tension and relieve headaches, backaches, and insomnia). Exercise releases the body's own painkillers called endorphins into your system. It makes you feel more in control, and gain a sense of emotional well-being.

❖ For men, exercise combats impotence, because of increased circulation to the reproductive organ. Exercise regularly if you are a man who suffers from impotence.

❖ Exercise encourages overall well-being.

❖ For couples, exercise improves your intimate life (libido).

❖ Exercise improves oxygen and nutrient supply to all cells in your body.

❖ Exercise helps prevent stroke.

❖ Exercise allows you to improve muscle strength, joint function, and joint structure.

❖ Exercise helps manage arthritis. Regular intensive exercise builds muscle strength and aerobic capacity, improves the ability to do daily tasks, and fosters a sense of well-being.

Tip: After a workout session at the gym, try hitting the sauna or steam room for a couple of minutes. It helps relax your muscles and soothe aches in both muscles and joints. Saunas relieve stress and help your body excrete toxins. Actually, this is the best way to help your body excrete excess toxins (lead, copper, zinc, nickel, and mercury). Saunas help cleanse the skin and promote faster healing of wounds on skin. Saunas help burn calories, fight illnesses, induce deeper sleep, improve cardiovascular performance, and they just feel good.

Get Enough Rest!

Psalm 4:8

New King James Version (NKJV)

I will both lie down in peace, and sleep;
For You alone, O LORD, make me dwell in safety.

Getting enough rest is as important as eating healthy and exercising. A well-rested body can cope well under pressure, and generally performs better in all aspects of life. When you rest, your body recuperates and damaged body cells are repaired, amongst a host of other things. Make sure that before you go to bed, you take time to wind down and just relax as you get in the mood for sleeping. Find a novel to read or listen to soothing music (especially if you have trouble sleeping at night). Using the sauna and steam room regularly not only detoxifies your body and improves skin tone and natural appearance, but can also improve your sleeping pattern. I'm talking from experience and not from research. Go for regular massage therapies if it helps with your sleep cycle. When you get enough hours to sleep at night (between 7 and 8 hours), you wake up more refreshed and energised and are more alert and less error-prone, especially at work. People who usually suffer from insomnia (which is a sleeping disorder) are grumpy, impatient, and moody. Even their metabolism is sluggish, they always feel tired and sleepy during the day, and their emotions are usually unstable. Look out for these symptoms, and adjust accordingly.

Health benefits of sufficient rest:

- ❖ Improves overall well-being and helps steer clear of depression
- ❖ Helps you avoid making accidents on the road; lack of rest affects your driving ability, and reduces concentration.
- ❖ Rest can help lower stress, thus improving blood pressure control and cardiovascular health.

❖ Getting enough rest helps with weight loss!! Believe it or not. Lack of it can cause changes in hormones that increase your appetite. You may also crave foods high in calories and carbohydrates to give you lost energy, which can contribute to weight gain.

❖ Helps sharpen attention and focus. It's amazing how rest affects our brain.

❖ For students, it improves your grades. Lack of sleep impairs your learning abilities.

❖ Improves overall performance. This is good news for athletes and performers: The more you rest, the better you perform. This applies to musicians and singers: Your body is your instrument (not just the vocal chords); your vocal chords are going to reflect the state of your body; and if your body is tired, then your voice will be tired, too.

❖ It helps spur creativity. In addition to consolidating memories, or making them stronger when sleeping, your brain appears to reorganise and restructure them as well, which may result in more creativity. The emotional components of a memory are strengthened during sleep, which helps spur the creativity process.

❖ Helps curb inflammation. Inflammation is linked to heart disease, diabetes, stroke, arthritis, and premature ageing. People who sleep six or fewer hours at night, have higher blood levels of inflammatory proteins than those who get more sleep.

❖ Just the right amount of sleeping hours per night can help you live longer – not too much and not too little. Sleep affects the quality of life. If you sleep better, you can certainly live better.

❖ Helps improve memory. During sleep, you can strengthen memories or "practise skills" learned while you were awake (consolidation). In other words, if you are trying to learn something new, you will perform better after sleep.

Go ahead and snooze for a bit! Watch out for sleep robbers, like stress and anxiety, caffeine (it can remain in the body for up to 20 hours), cigarettes and alcohol, medications, too much sugar and highly processed foods, low-carb diets, excessive exercise (especially 3 hours before sleep), a bad mattress or pillow, a snoring spouse, hot flashes, enlarged prostate, new-born babies, environment, and painful physical conditions, like arthritis, tendonitis, chronic back pain, and so forth. Lack of enough sleep causes our bodies to become acidic (especially if it's less than 6 hours), and we know that our bodies under-perform under such unhealthy conditions.

Rest is not only in terms of sleeping, but also abstaining from any form of labour or work, and taking the time to just relax and just be. In Genesis 2:1-3, God rested from *"all His work He had done."* He had spent six days in creation, and on the seventh day He rested. He made the seventh day Holy and a day of rest, and He commanded the children of Israel to observe the same (Exodus 20:8-11). Notice that not even the animals were to do any form of manual labour, they were also to rest and observe the Sabbath. And in Leviticus 25, six years the children of Israel were to work their fields, prune their vineyards and gather the fruits; but in the seventh year, there was to be a Sabbath of solemn rest for the land. They were to neither sow their fields, nor prune their vineyards. The land was to *"furnish"* food for them and their families without anyone touching it. According to Leviticus 25:21-22, the Lord was to command a *"special"* blessing on the children of Israel so that their land would produce enough fruit for threes year, since they were to only start sowing in the eight year and reap in the ninth year. Just reading from all these scriptures, it is clear to see that God Himself, our creator, ordained *"rest."* It is not good for a man or woman to work tirelessly without taking some time to rest. God as our *manufacturer* requires that we rest and have some time to recuperate. This is to our benefit, because it is in resting that we will become more fruitful and productive, for one who works continuously without rest is like a ticking time bomb, and one day the bomb will *set off*! (Explode). Notice that any of the children of Israel who were to break this *command* to rest, they were to be cut-off from their people, and their inheritance. This is how serious this matter was to God. It was a command, and not an option (*Our manufacturer knows best, for He created us*). If He himself (God) rested after six days of productivity, then we should learn from Our Father and Creator, besides He simply instructed us to follow His example.

So I say, go ahead and take that long deserved break. Go on a holiday, take some time off and spend time with family and friends. Learn to just relax, taking the moment in, and just be grateful for life and all your achievements. For God looked back at what He had created for six days, and He saw that it was *good*. Take the time to just appreciate God (*for He is the one who gives us strength to get wealth*), and the labour/ work of your hands. Rest, but let not your rest be an excuse to become lazy (Proverbs 6:10-11), for rest is only for the one who is working and doing something productive. Everything is to be done in moderation, and in the right time. Observe rest!

Purpose in your heart to eat healthy, stay healthy, and lead a healthy lifestyle!

TRUE WHOLENESS

Have the fruit of the Spirit

Galatians 5:22–23

Amplified Bible (AMP)

But the fruit of the [Holy] Spirit [the work which His presence within accomplishes] is love, joy (gladness), peace, patience (an even temper, forbearance), kindness, goodness (benevolence), faithfulness, Gentleness (meekness, humility), self-control (self-restraint, continence). Against such things there is no law [that can bring a charge].

What defines true wholeness? How can one measure a person's wholeness? What are the characteristics of a truly whole person? Wholeness cannot be measured by the degrees you have, the wealth you possess, the cars you drive, the clothes you wear, or the type of job or career you are in. For many have such but still live miserably. They have no joy and no peace of mind because the one who gives it all does not reside in them. So what is true wholeness then?

True wholeness can only be achieved when you've got the Spirit of God in you, when you've got the one who is the peace giver Himself in you, and we can tell by the fruit you produce, which are love, joy, peace, longsuffering, gentleness, goodness, faith, meekness, and temperance. For these are the fruit of the Spirit, the characteristics that define a truly whole person. You can have all the world offers, but without the fruit of the Spirit, you are not yet living a fulfilled life as you should.

Add the fruit of the Spirit to your lifestyle, and you'll see how fulfilling your life will be. Ask the one who gives it all to be in you, because when you have the Spirit of wisdom in you, then you have it all.

Principle #8:

LOVE OUT LOUD

There is no greater Love than this; that you lay down your life for others.
—Jesus Christ

Love heals; love forgives; love gives; love is caring and considerate; love is gentle and kind; love never fails! Love is the major key to success in life spiritually and physically. Without love, we are good as nothing. The love factor is what makes us resist ill feelings towards others. When you have true genuine love, it is impossible to become spiteful or jealous of other people. When you have true genuine love, you celebrate others. When you have true genuine love, nothing and no one intimidates you and you are always at peace. When you have true agape love, you let go of the urge to be revengeful. Love can never breed evil thoughts and actions; if anything, it dissolves them. Decide this day to be a prisoner of love. When you are a prisoner, the chains that bind you constrain you and keep you under control. Let love be like the chains that constrain a prisoner. When you are full of it, there is no place for hatred towards others in your heart. When you are full of it, it controls the way you behave and treat others. When you are bound by the chains of love, you become a servant of love, bound under its principles, and your actions are evidence of that great force that controls you from within. Let's look at love according to the definition of the Bible, from that famous Scripture 1 Corinthians 13. For this is the way that love should be in all its perfection.

1 Corinthians 13:4–8

Amplified Bible (AMP)

*Love endures long and is patient and kind; love
never is envious nor boils over with jealousy, is not
boastful or vainglorious, does not display itself haughtily.
It is not conceited (arrogant and inflated with pride); it is not rude
(unmannerly) and does not act unbecomingly. Love (God's love in
us) does not insist on its own rights or its own way, for it is not self-
seeking; it is not touchy or fretful or resentful; it takes no account
of the evil done to it [it pays no attention to a suffered wrong].
It does not rejoice at injustice and unrighteousness,
but rejoices when right and truth prevail.
Love bears up under anything and everything that comes, is ever
ready to believe the best of every person, its hopes are fadeless under
all circumstances, and it endures everything [without weakening].
Love never fails [never fades out or becomes obsolete or comes to
an end]. As for prophecy (the gift of interpreting the divine will
and purpose), it will be fulfilled and pass away; as for tongues,
they will be destroyed and cease; as for knowledge, it will pass
away [it will lose its value and be superseded by truth].*

Love is a beautiful emotion that has positive effects when expressed correctly and genuinely. The Bible instructs us to love God first, with all our heart, mind, soul, and strength, and then to love each other as we love ourselves. The question is, Do you love yourself? People who always fault find and criticise themselves will always have problems loving others, because the way they treat themselves is the way they will most likely treat others.

True genuine love heals, and it puts joy in someone else's heart. Or should I say true acts of compassion and kindness have got a healing effect on the soul. Not only will others be healed through love, but you also heal yourself when you love. It's like a boomerang effect; healing is thrown back to the love thrower and both parties benefit. Whether the other person loves you or not is their problem. When you love, you become like your Father in heaven who is love Himself. Look at how He causes the sun to shine on both the good and evil; He is impartial. There are many people out there who need just a little bit of compassion, a little bit of care, a little bit of gentleness, and someone just to talk to. Why not be the one to give out that beautiful expression called love. I dare you to go out there today and put a smile on someone else's face by just showing acts of kindness towards them. Be a good listener; take time to listen to someone else's story; be genuinely interested in people and give of your time.

Love always seeks to do well to others; it is not selfish (like Scripture says), and they say, sharing is caring. How often do we share of what we have with others? True love always seeks to help others without gain. How many people can you count and say, I have helped them without expecting anything in return? One thing I've come to discover in life is that we were put on this earth for someone else's benefit. God created me to be of great help to someone else. I've got something in me that others need to benefit from; that's the whole purpose of life. But somehow, selfishness has crept into the hearts of countless souls, thus forming a cancer of self-centeredness, which slows down execution of purpose, fruitfulness, and rate of success. Loving others is very important; when you have unconditional love, you can never be selfish! Now use the portion of Scripture as a thermometer to measure your love towards others and then try and rectify where you fall short. Note how the Bible says, "Love never fails". This is very true. Even when people are being rude, spiteful, and hurtful towards you, Scripture says, keep loving them, because by so doing, it's like you are heaping coals of fire on top of their heads. One day they will turn around and start to treat you with the same love you have shown them. Trust me, you will gain much respect from the same people who used to give you grief if you are just consistent with your love towards them, even though it might be painful. Let me show you this story:

Once a man had stopped by a river bank to drink water. There he saw a scorpion floundering in the water, and he decided to save it by stretching out his finger. The scorpion stung him, but the man persisted in trying to save the scorpion from drowning. A man standing nearby tried to discourage him from saving the scorpion, because it seems like it kept stinging him with every attempt. But the man being stung replied and said, "It's the nature of the scorpion to sting, but it is also my nature to love. Why should I give up my nature to love just because of the nature of the scorpion to sting?"

This story has stuck by me ever since someone sent that to my phone. People around you may be like scorpions, always stinging you, but don't give up your nature to love! Let the fruit of love abound in you and let your actions be evidence of the love you possess inside. When you are full of it, it surely controls you, and we will be able to see the evidence.

Greek definitions of love:

 # Eros: As the name denotes, eros can be referred to as a love that has to do with physical passion. It is mostly sexual and carnal in nature. Everything erotic comes from this kind of love. It's simply the pleasure and gratification of the flesh, and it's usually enjoyed between married couples. However the Greeks say, eros does not have to be sexual in nature. It can be that attraction or connection between two people where sex is not of concern. The connection is of a much deeper kind than that of just companions. It is a type of love but still not the "perfect" kind of love.

 # Philia: Philia is the love between friends, and friendship is described as a strong bond between people who share common interest or activity. Philia is the kind of love that delights and longs to be in the presence of another, a warm feeling that comes and goes with intensity. They say philia is freely chosen. It has got nothing to do with biological connection, because the bond can override family or biological connections. Hence you find some friends who are much closer to each other than they are with their own biological family members. A good example of philia is the love between David and Jonathan. David and Jonathan are a lost art in modern days, such love is rare to find nowadays. The Bible says their hearts where "knit" together (1 Samuel 18:1–4), and they loved each other as they loved their own souls. In ancient times, it was described as the happiest and most fully human of all loves, the crown of life, and the school of virtue. It's sad that the modern world ignores it. (One touching thing about David and Jonathan's account of love is that, even after Jonathan had long died, David remained faithful to his friend and "brother" by looking after Jonathan's only remaining child Mephibosheth until he died). And yet, there is still a greater kind of love that can perfect philia. (I would like to think that the love between David and Jonathan was already perfected by agape love. David never broke the covenant he made with Jonathan even though Jonathan's father, Saul, sought to kill David. David remained loyal to Jonathan, even after Jonathan's death. If people would only love each other so diligently.)

Storge: Storge or natural affection is described as fondness through familiarity. It's known as a brotherly love, expresses mere acceptance, and "puts up" with situations. This love is shared between family members or people who have found themselves by chance. Not the best kind of love, because the affection can be conditional. It is liable to go bad and can be affected by jealousy and corruption if not careful.

Agape: This love is defined as divine and spiritual, not part of human nature naturally (hence why it has to be practised or exercised so that it becomes a part of us). A love so rich and deep and most importantly unconditional, with no limits or boundaries. This is God's kind of love towards us, and He expects us to love each other the same way He unconditionally loves us. I love to call agape the "perfected love", because out of all the different kinds of love, this one is the ultimate, it the best form of love and the one I'm making reference to on this principle. It is not based on how you feel about the next person; you still love them regardless of how they treat you! God commands this kind of love towards each other out of duty and service to one another. Agape love transcends and perfects the other three types of love. The other kinds of love without agape will at some point result in disappointment,

heartbreak, resentment, and so forth. However, agape love remains constant; it's unchanging, unmovable, and unshakable; it's like love built on a rock (the winds may come, the storms may rage, but it will never move an inch). Agape love must be the rod that holds together and natures and nourishes the three other kinds of love. Without this rod of agape love, everything else is bound to fall apart!

No Greater Love

When you find it in your heart to care deeply for someone else, then you would have succeeded.
—Dr Maya Angelou

Scripture states that there is no greater love than to lay down one's life for others. That got me thinking! Ask yourself, Have I ever laid down my life for someone? Have I ever given of myself selflessly to someone so that I could be there for them and meet their needs? As we all know, love is a "doing" word. And usually the fruit of genuine unconditional love are shown through acts of kindness, compassion, care, patience, and giving. When you love, you give. Giving is not only in terms of material things but also in terms of time, advice, and counsel. Give your life wholly to someone else's advantage. What a change it will make in this world. Ask yourself, How deep does my love reach?

Do something for someone who will never be able to repay you!

I like to think of love as a muscle. The more you exercise it and nourish it, the more it grows. Now go on and build that muscle of love, walk in love today, and help transform your life and others around you. People might forget the things you do for them, but they will never forget how you make them feel! Come on, make someone feel loved, and be genuine and sincere because it will show. Endeavour to help someone live a better life. When God has put love and compassion in your heart for someone else, don't ignore that love but pursue it, because that person needs what you have! When you love, you become complete. I believe that when God said we should be perfect, He was referring to the way we love each other. It's only in love that we are perfected. And perfect love casts out all fear!

Ambassadors of Christ

2 Corinthians 5:20
KJV (King James Version)
Now then we are ambassadors for Christ, as though God did beseech you by us: we pray you in Christ's stead, be ye reconciled to God.

Many Christians claim to be ambassadors of Christ and yet ignore the ambassadorial duties of an ambassador. Some do not even know the role of an ambassador! Our duty as ambassadors of Christ is to represent Christ and His kingdom, which is the kingdom of heaven. As ambassadors of Christ, it is our duty to uphold the government's principles, adhering to heaven's code of conduct, living by its values, displaying the culture of our home country (heaven), and speaking the mind of our King wherever we go, so that those who see us will not question where our allegiances lie. Look at Jesus before all power and authority was given to Him. He was about God's business when He was on earth; He only spoke and executed the will of the Father. Conveying only God's opinion was Christ duty. He even said that the words that he spoke were not His own but His Father's words, because He understood that, as an ambassador, His personal opinion did not matter. Only the Father's opinion was to be aired. He was one with the Father because He lived and breathed God's will alone and nothing else. His heartbeat was in sync with heartbeat of God.

Ambassadors in general terms are special envoys, highest ranking diplomats accredited to another sovereign state to represent the government they come from. They have plenipotentiary powers (i.e., full authority to represent the government). Their duty is to uphold the principles, culture, and values of the country they come from. When you see an ambassador, even when you visit their home, everything about them represents the government they come from, even their dressing, language, conduct, and so forth. Ambassadors who fail to represent their government are recalled because they have failed in their duties.

Since Christ is our sovereign, our duty is to represent Him and His government well, and our allegiance should be to Him alone and His sovereignty. So when I say I'm Christ's ambassador, do I really mean what I confess? My character/behaviour should support my claim. Let it not just be word of mouth, but let my actions affirm my confessions. Everything about me should scream "Christ" from every angle.

"A new commandment I give unto you; that you love one another as I have loved you. By this shall all man know that you are my disciples, if you have love one for another" (John 13:34–35). True ambassadors of Christ are identified by the attitude of love they show to others around them. One who is totally controlled by the love of Christ, like I said, behaves like described in 1 Corinthians 13. Love is the greatest commandment, and it embodies the other commandments given before Christ came. Love is the centre of Christian living, and the rod where everything else hangs, because where there is no love, everything else falls apart. (Matthew 22:36–40). There is no way you can be led to kill or dishonour someone when you have true love. When you are full of it, love controls your speech and behaviour. You simply avoid causing offence to the ones dear at heart; everything you do supports the next person's interests.

Think of how Christ loved us. He had to die for us; everything He did was in our interest and for our benefit. Now that's love! Our duty is just to demonstrate the love of Christ, regardless of a person's age, background, sexual orientation, culture, or nationality. We are simply commissioned to love and never to judge. Judging should be left to God alone. Our opinion towards certain issues and matters do not matter to God. We should only be concerned with loving everyone unconditionally without prejudice. Let's see if you can pass that test.

Loving someone does not mean you endorse any negative attributes they might have. It simply means that you are giving the person a chance to get things right and in order, no matter how long it might take the person. After all, love is patient and long-suffering, kind, and never rude. Christ died for everyone on the cross (John 3:16). In doing so, He demonstrated love in all its perfection. He did not choose whom to die for or whom not to die for. He simply obeyed the Father's command and will and gave everyone the same chance to enter heaven if they are willing to yield to the rulership of God.

Hatred Is a Burden I Choose Not to Carry

In John 4:20, John, the apostle of love, poses a question: "If a man says he loves God, and yet hates his brother whom he sees, he is a liar. For how can he love God whom He has not seen?" Walking in hatred is walking in darkness. How deep is that darkness that surrounds you? The opposite is true about love. When you walk in it, you walk in light, your path is illuminated, and you see where you are going. Walking in hatred only supports the kingdom of darkness, and you become its perfect ambassador, because you uphold its morals of hatred.

When love is perfected in you, nothing causes you to stumble and fall because light shines in your path, unlike when you are walking in darkness. Love is like the oil that keeps the lamp burning in your soul. When your soul is full of light, everything about life is bright and beautiful; you are pleasant to be around and a breath of fresh air. Many are attracted to the light beaming from within your heart, and they find comfort and peace in your presence. No good fruit comes from an evil soul encompassed with darkness all around! I liken hatred towards others to a garbage bin with rotting waste, producing smell and everything unpleasant, at the same time attracting flies and all sorts of unpleasantness. Both love and hatred attract something; one attracts the positive, and the other attracts the negative. Choose this day to just love without prejudice. You lose nothing but gain everything! The Bible says that, in the end, the love of many shall grow cold. They will call you weird and all sorts of names just because you choose to walk in love. Please do not be counted in that number that has grown cold. Resist the temptation to yield and give in to their scornful words and mocking views. Develop thick skin against such and choose to stay in the light! As much as we celebrate "eros" love on Valentine's Day, it is more important to celebrate *"agape"* love everyday as a lifestyle, for without it we are nothing. All the other types of love have their limits, but agape love is perfect and without conditions. It transcends feelings, and looks past one's faults. It is always believing, always hopeful, and it loves without judgement, prejudice, or condemnation. It loves *"in spite of,"* reaches out *"despite of,"* and it cares *"irregardless of."* Indeed it is the perfected kind of love. For without faith, it is impossible to please God *(Hebrews 11:6)*, but without love it is equally impossible to please God either. For your faith will fail if you don't have love *(1 Corinthians 13:2)*, and you are counted as nothing. Love adds value to your very being and existence, it is what makes you and everything that you do count before God, and before men. It is what sets you apart from the ordinary man. It is the crown of life! So these three remain; faith, hope and love. But the greatest of these is love, for there is no greater force or power than that of love. *(1 Corinthians 13:13)*. Love God our Father first and then love your neighbour as yourself, for these are the greatest commandments.

Love like you will never get the chance again! Don't be afraid to express this beautiful emotion. True love has no barriers or limits, it cuts through the toughest of walls and heals the soul. It remains constant in every season of life!
—David Conellias

Purpose in your heart to be a prisoner of Love!

Principle #9:

FORGIVE AND ASK FOR FORGIVENESS

Harboured hatred is like acid that eats your soul and body away! Release that acid by forgiving.
—David Conellias

Forgiveness is one of the toughest for some and yet the most liberating thing to do. People who are proud and pompous usually struggle to forgive others. Some define forgiveness as letting go of the pressing desire to revenge. When you harbour hatred in your heart towards someone, it's like you have created a jail cell in your heart and locked that person inside. Now the question is, how many people have you locked up? And for how long? I believe unforgiveness and hatred not only eats away your soul like acid, but it also blocks God's blessing into your life. Some of our major breakthroughs in life are dependent on our forgiveness towards others! If you still harbour hatred and resentment towards others, if you are still hateful and spiteful towards your neighbour, then you are blocking your own progress in life and also affecting your personal health, as I shall show you. It is up to you to go and make amends, fix what has been broken, and pursue the path to total healing and complete forgiveness. When you free the ones who hurt you, you also free yourself from carrying unnecessary baggage in your heart. You need to forgive not only others but also yourself. Don't be too hard on yourself when you miss the mark or when you don't achieve a goal. Learn to forgive yourself and move on. When you ask for God to forgive you, believe that you are forgiven as long as you forgive the next person as well. *Forgive me, Lord, as I also forgive others.* For how can God forgive you, if you can't forgive others? Here the law of reciprocity applies! Not only does unforgiveness impede progress in your life, it prevents you from entering heaven! If Christ's mission was to come here on earth to die for the sins of the world, so that the world could be forgiven and reconciled back to God; then who are we to not forgive our neighbour when they wrong us, yet Christ had to suffer for our own forgiveness? This is a serious matter to God *(Matthew 6:14-15)*, God will only forgive you of your trespasses when you forgive others as well, there are no negotiations, no exceptions, and no conditions, it doesn't matter how deeply the next person hurt you, you have to find a way to forgive them, just as you would want God to forgive you when you have committed the gravest of sins. The true mark of maturity is when somebody hurts you and you try to understand their situation instead of trying to hurt them back.

Luke 6:37
New King James Version (NKJV)

Judge not, and you shall not be judged. Condemn not, and you shall not be condemned. Forgive, and you will be forgiven.

Be Merciful

Proverbs 3:3
Amplified Bible (AMP)

Let not mercy and kindness [shutting out all hatred and selfishness] and truth [shutting out all deliberate hypocrisy or falsehood] forsake you; bind them about your neck, write them upon the tablet of your heart.

We are instructed again, to bind mercy, kindness, and truth around our necks, and to write them on the tablet of our hearts. Now when something is bound on your neck, no one can take it off you except you. Everybody can see it; it's exposed. When it's written on the tablet of your heart, it's meant to stay and stick on you, like a memorial, to remind you of how merciful God has been to you as well. When something is at heart, you are always thinking about it 24/7; it's a part of your life. Often times we ask God to show us mercy, but how often do we show mercy to others? It's like we forget that Scripture that talks about us obtaining mercy when we show mercy to others (Matthew 5:7). When you show mercy to others, you have every right to ask for mercy from God and receive the same compassion you have shown to others. You have every right to ask God to "blot out" your transgressions. When something is blotted out, it is removed completely from recognition or memory, just like you use bleach to blot out a stain on a white piece of cloth. It would be as if you never sinned in the first place. The blood of Jesus Christ is the best bleaching agent that blots out our sin, and our forgiveness towards others is the key that unlocks the "bleaching" and "cleansing" power of the blood of Christ.

Matthew 5:7

Amplified Bible (AMP)

Blessed (happy, to be envied, and spiritually prosperous—with life-joy and satisfaction in God's favour and salvation, regardless of their outward conditions) are the merciful, for they shall obtain mercy!

Even as Christ forgave us of our trespasses, we should also forgive others their debts. When we forgive first, then God in turn forgives us as well.

Ask for Forgiveness

Meekness is not weakness.

—Dr Walter Masocha

Ask for forgiveness from God and, when you offend others, ask for their forgiveness too. Never conceal your sin from God; it hinders your prosperity as well as much as unforgiveness (Proverbs 28:13). When you confess and renounce your sins you obtain mercy from God. He is a just and merciful God. Don't be too proud to ask for forgiveness. It is only the bravest of persons who asks for forgiveness when they have wronged their brother or sister, or have been wronged themselves. A mature person is quick to realise their fault, rectify, and ask for forgiveness.

Asking for forgiveness from your brother even when you are not at fault shows the fruit of meekness in you. People always think meek people are weak. A meek person possesses wisdom, they know when to answer and when to keep their mouths shut, and they know how to respond and how not to respond. Now that's controlled strength. Meekness is not weakness but strength under control; otherwise, if it wasn't under control, it would wreak havoc. In most cases, the meek are usually the ones to ask for forgiveness first, and I commend such people. By asking for forgiveness, you won't lose anything but actually gain a sense of freedom by freeing your soul of unnecessary garbage.

Matthew 5:5

Amplified Bible (AMP)

Blessed (happy, blithesome, joyous, spiritually prosperous—
with life-joy and satisfaction in God's favour and salvation,
regardless of their outward conditions) are the meek (the mild,
patient, long-suffering), for they shall inherit the earth!

Effects of Unforgiveness and Bitterness on Our health:

* ❖ Higher rates of heart disease and cardiac arrest
* ❖ Elevated blood pressure
* ❖ Stomach ulcers
* ❖ Arthritis
* ❖ Back problems
* ❖ Headaches and chronic pain

Unforgiveness and bitterness are like a cancer of the soul. When someone hurts you or offends you, the Bible says, go to the person, try and speak to them, and rectify the situation rather than harbouring resentment. You could save yourself a lot of trouble by being humble enough to talk it out with the person and then choosing to forgive them anyway, regardless of them apologizing. It's you who benefits in the end. It does not matter if the person decides to carry on with the grudge, but at least you have done your part. In your pursuit to obtain forgiveness from your brother, your main aim is to win them back. Don't say words that further aggravate or exacerbate the situation; let your words be the water that quenches the fire and make it die out. (Read Matthew 18:15–35.) Forgiveness is one of the major principles in the kingdom of heaven. Choose today to forgive, and when you forgive, you find that your life improves! It doesn't matter if the person keeps on repeating the same mistake. When you are merciful, you are patient with the person. When you have love, according to 1 Corinthians 13, you are always forgiving, always kind, not easily provoked, you bare all things and are long suffering, you keep hope alive that maybe one day the person who keeps wronging you will change. Put an effort to make things right with the next person and then move on from there.

I leave you with 1 Peter 4:8: "Above all things have intense and unfailing love for one another, for love covers a multitude of sins [forgives and disregards the offenses of others]."

Purpose in your heart to forgive, and to be a peacemaker!

Principle #10:

JUST BE JOYFUL, SMILE, AND TAKE TIME TO LAUGH

A merry heart doeth good like medicine, but
a broken spirit drieth the bones.
—King Solomon

I have come to learn the difference between being happy and having joy. Happiness is short-lived and circumstantial, but joy has no condition and does not rely on circumstances. I believe joy and peace go hand in hand, because when you have joy, you are at peace, and when you have peace, you still remain joyful no matter what comes your way. Joy gives one strength to face challenges that come in life; it's the fuel that keeps one going when others cave in. Just like love, having joy can be healing.

LOL (Laugh Out Loud)

Take time out to laugh, have a bit of humour, and don't be too serious. "It does good like medicine", the Bible says in Proverbs 17:22. Some even say laughter is the best medicine, and I agree. Complete that joy by creating moments to laugh with others. They say the sound of laughter is much more contagious than a cough or sneeze! It improves memory, strengthens our immune system, boosts energy, diminishes pain, and is a powerful antidote to stress. It lightens burdens, inspires hope, and keeps you grounded, focused, and alert. Take time to even laugh at yourself; share your embarrassing moments with others. Spend more time with those people who make you laugh the most. I call them "the natural painkillers". Have a natural painkiller handy when you need one during difficult moments in life. When laughter is shared, it binds people together, increasing happiness, joy, and intimacy. It triggers healthy physical changes in our bodies. To top it up, laughter is the best form of medicine for the mind and body, and it's free. You only need to make it happen!

Benefits of hearty laughter:

❖ It protects your heart by improving the function of blood vessels and increasing blood flow, which can help protect you against heart attack and other cardiovascular problems. Your organs in general (heart, brain, and lungs) are energised and stimulated into action because of increased blood flow.

❖ It impacts blood sugar levels.

❖ It provides a burst of exercise.

❖ It relaxes your muscles by relieving physical tension and stress, leaving muscles relaxed for up to 45 minutes thereafter.

❖ It is believed to aid in digestion as well.

❖ It boosts immune system by decreasing stress hormones and increasing immune cells and infection-fighting antibodies, thereby increasing resistance to disease.

❖ It triggers release of the body's natural feel-good chemicals endorphins. Endorphins promote an overall sense of well-being and can temporarily relieve pain.

❖ Hearty laughter adds joy and zest to life.

❖ It eases anxiety and fear, thus helping shift perspective. It allows you to see situations in a more realistic, less threatening light. A humorous perspective creates psychological distance, which helps avoid feeling overwhelmed.

❖ It improves mood and enhances resilience (the capacity to recover quickly from difficulties). It dissolves distressing emotions; you can't feel anxious, angry, or sad when you are laughing. Use humour and play to overcome challenges and enhance your life.

❖ It strengthens relationships, keeping them fresh and exciting. If you want stronger and healthier relationships, then learn to laugh out loud with your loved ones and people in your circle.

Laughter unites people during difficult times and is a powerful effective way to heal resentments, hurts, and disagreements.

❖ When you are full of humour, you become spontaneous.

❖ It attracts others to us. Nobody wants to be around a grumpy person; people enjoy the company of a joyful person. A joyful person exudes warmth from within, thus affecting people around them. When you are humorous, you make more friends.

❖ It promotes group bonding, enhancing team work, and helps defuse conflict.

❖ Laughter helps you forget judgements, criticism, and doubts.

❖ It helps relieve inhibitions; your fear of holding back and holding on are set back.

❖ It helps coping skills. You cope much better when under pressure or faced with a challenge just by laughing

❖ Deeply felt emotions are allowed to rise to the surface.

Never be too busy to laugh; it's only you who suffers!

You Look So Much Better When You Smile

When you see a person without a smile, give them one of yours.
—Zig Ziglar

Learn to smile, even when greeting someone; it warms up the next person's heart. When you smile at people genuinely (we know when it's fake), they feel more welcome and are at ease with you. A simple genuine and heartily smile can go a long way, especially when trying to build relationships with people. Learn to smile even when there's nothing to smile about. Force that smile on your face; it will change your mood from the inside out. Smiling triggers activity in your brain. There's a serious mind-body connection, in your left frontal cortex to be exact, which is an area in your brain that registers joy and happiness.

Have you ever heard the song by Louis Armstrong *When You Smile, the Whole World Smiles With You*? It's been proven that when you smile, yes, everybody around you smiles as well, even if they didn't want to, and I can vouch for that because I've observed it too. Smiling is definitely contagious, just like laughter because both are more or less the same. When you are around someone who is feeling good, that feeling is bound to catch on to you as well. Why not be the one who passes around the feel-good mood to everybody around you. Smiling eventually leads to laughter. Smiling makes someone more attractive, and just like laughter, it helps relieve stress. Smiling can even help you get a job because it makes you more likable. Smiling strongly makes you feel good. Just try it, especially when you are feeling down and low. The moment you smile, or find something to smile about, it improves your mood.

Purpose in your heart to always be joyful no matter what!
Put on the garment of praise, and let your heart rejoice,
chasing away the spirit of heaviness. (Isaiah 61:3)

Principle #11:

BE AUTHENTIC, DARE TO STAND OUT, REVEAL THE GLORY

You were designed for accomplishment, engineered for
success, and endowed with seeds of greatness.
—Zig Ziglar

To be authentic simply means to be of undisputed origin, and not a copy but genuine. You are original, real, true, veritable, sterling, undisputed, rightful, lawful, legal, or valid. God put us here on earth to reveal His glory through our authentic selves. When you look at a flower, its glory is in the petals and the beautiful array of colours we behold. The same is with us; we are like that flower that needs to elaborately spread out its petals for others to admire and marvel at the glory of God being expressed. How can I express the glory of God within me? The answer is simple: by being authentic! Choose to be an elaborate, powerful, and influential force of nature. Know that you were pre-ordained by God to become the best that you could ever allow yourself to be. Your ordination does not need people to gather around you and re-affirm what God has already confirmed in you! No man needs to approve of you, you are already approved of by God and that's a done deal. Stop wasting time seeking man's approval.

Genetics

God has intrinsically designed each and every one of us with a unique genetic code. Ever wondered why each and every single person on this planet has got different finger prints? No one's finger prints are the same, because you were never meant to be a clone of someone, but an original, intricate and rich in every detail. Look at fraternal (dizygotic) twins. You might dress them up the same, take them to the same school, involve them in the same sport, but as they grow older, their true opposing identities begin to surface in their characteristics and the way they behave. You'll find that one might develop a taste for cooking, and then the other might absolutely hate cooking but have a taste for aesthetics. But more interestingly, look at monozygotic (identical) twins. Monozygotic twins are definitely identical but not entirely. Their genetic makeup has a "slight" variance. This variance is the defining point of their authenticity. Identical twins also have different fingerprints, just like everybody else, even though they came from one zygote, and possibly shared the same placenta.

Monozygotic twins develop different phenotypes (observable physical or biochemical characteristics, as determined both by genetic makeup and environmental influences; the expression of a specific trait, such as stature or blood type, based on genetic and environmental influences). Despite having the same genotype, monozygotic twins are genetically not entirely the same. It is estimated that, on average, a set of monozygotic twins will have about 360 genetic differences that occurred very early in foetal development. These genetic differences will be present in nearly every cell in the body.

If we can learn this truth about the slight variance in identical twins, are we being original, just as God has designed us to be? God makes even the monozygotic twins genotype and phenotype slightly differ. Even though they might have many similar characteristics, there's always bound to be that variance that sets apart one from the other. This is a clear sign of how God values and emphasises the uniqueness of each of His creation.

Everybody is meant to bring something different and unique to the table. This is what makes this world a colourful place. Even in monozygotic twins, one might be a gifted musician, and the other a gifted footballer. Imagine the monotony; if we were all singers, music would eventually become boring! God intentionally made everything about nature dynamic, so that we could enjoy the beauty of colour. The differences in characteristics, behaviour, and gifting are meant for us to complement each other, and not keep us apart. They are meant for us to serve one another within our different areas of strength. I might possess a quality that could prove beneficial and profitable to my dear companion, friend, or colleague. It is like pieces of a puzzle; each piece is different in shape and size, but it's meant to fit into God's beautiful tapestry, thus creating a masterpiece.

Spiritual Matters

When we adopt God's character and behaviour (His way of doing things) first, we find that our own individual authenticity is perfected. When I make a decision to be God-like (by choice), when I possess the fruit of the Spirit, when I allow Christ to be the centre of my being and become one with Him, I flourish in my authenticity and an anointing is added to my abilities, which makes me stand out even more!

In your pursuit to authenticity, don't lose or sell your soul. Don't lose the real you that God has meant you to be (the very essence of you, your Godly character as His child, and everything that truly makes you who you are in Christ). Mark 8:36 says, "What shall it profit a man, if he shall gain the whole world, and lose his soul?" Do not let the world and its corrupt ways buy your soul by defining what it supposedly thinks you should be. We are in this world but not of this world. Stick to God's standards like the good ambassador in Christ that you are. Let God's standards govern the very essence of your being.

Excavate! What Is Your Call?

Matthew 25:15

King James Version (KJV)

And unto one he gave five talents, to another two, and
to another one; to every man according to his several
ability; and straightway took his journey.

Talents

We were blessed with different gifts and talents on different levels and degrees. Even when it comes to having the same gifts, we can both be singers, but my level or capacity of gifting is slightly different in delivery from another singer, according to my God given abilities. Gifts might be the same but different in style and genre when it comes to music production. Look at the story in Matthew 25:14–30. All three were given the same talents of gold, but with different measures according to their God-given abilities. What sets all three apart is their attitude towards what they had been given. The one who got two talents, went further and worked hard to produce two more to make them four. Same with one who got five; he went and doubled them to ten. The one who got one talent was lazy to better himself and expand on what he had been naturally given, and so he decided to do what lazy people do best – nothing! He actually wasted time and energy on digging the talent so as to hide it in the ground, when he could have used that talent to his advantage and betterment!

Even when it comes to gifts and talents in general, they are given to people in the same manner. I might not be able to necessarily emulate what the next person does, but that does not make me any less gifted. I should actually flourish in my capacity and strive to become better. Some are given a one-talent level of gifting, others a two-talent level of gifting, and still others a five-talent level of gifting. How far you go depends on how hard you work to develop yourself further. Don't become discouraged and burry your talent.

You can look at this story from different perspectives. The number of talents might also represent the number of gifts and abilities God has given you (jacket of many colours). You might find that when you start excavating the authentic you, you discover other hidden talents that are natural to you and then expand on what you already where familiar with. You might be familiar with three gifts you possess but in your excavation develop an interest for three other activities. I will talk about *cross networking* later on. The ones who discover other hidden talents are the ones who choose to do something with what they are already familiar with.

Excavate

God has designed everyone uniquely and encoded their true identity in their DNA. What you are meant to be is a hidden treasure inside of you, which can only be accessed and dug out by you! Some are lazy to simply excavate and pursue who they truly are; thus they copy someone else. Well let me tell you something: Being a copy of someone else is much more hard work than being the real you that God designed. Yes, excavation requires effort, but you'll find that in your excavation, you remove the unnecessary dirt that might have clogged up the hidden diamond inside. So in the end it's all worth it. Even relationships can be authentic and stand out, especially if there is a high degree of agreement and oneness among parties involved. It's a matter of knowing and choosing the right companions.

> *You were created to bring something to this earth that has never crystallised throughout the eons of time.*
> —T. D. Jakes

No Duplication

It is good to admire others and what they do, but in your admiration don't be caught up in duplication of identity. It is good to emulate good things that you see other gifted and talented people do, but it is also better to do it in your own unique way and learn to put your unique stamp to it. Pursue the things you are passionate about, even career-wise; do something that you enjoy doing, and you will find that you will prosper in that area. Put a touch of excellence to your work. Your work has to be admirable and desirable to the beholder. Don't settle for mediocrity but rise above it. Show the world not just your best but your excellent side. Let your works scream excellence at every angle.

> *Put your seal, your scent, your essence, your DNA, on what*
> *you produce, and it will forever have that uniqueness.*
> —T. D. Jakes

So I ask the question, What's your true unique identity? First of all, our identity as children of God is found in His Word and what He calls us, a royal priesthood, a peculiar (different from what is considered normal according to the standards of the world) people. Search the Scriptures, know what He calls you, and pronounce it and believe it. Once we know our identity in Christ, we ought to know what He has designed us to be. As children of God, we can be one and like-minded and share common beliefs. The difference only comes in the assignments we are meant to carry out and what we are designed for individually. Then again, you might come across people on the same assignment as you. The only difference will be how diligently you carry out your assignment, as compared to the next person who is on a similar track with you. But even though the assignment is the same, God gave you your own natural signature to stamp your work. Use that signature that sets you apart to mark your work and assignments.

What is it that makes you different and stand out from everybody else? What motivates you and drives you? What are the things that spark your interest? Is it your attention to detail or your love for fashion? Is it your innate musical ear or your love for aesthetics? Is it your love for automobiles or your love for sport? Is it wedding planning? Who are you meant to be? These are all questions that help us discover our true authentic selves. We should know what Christ calls us first through His word and then what He has designed us to be.

Express Yourself

*Being different isn't a bad thing, it means you
are brave enough to be yourself!*
—Unknown

Don't be afraid to stand out. You were never meant to fit into the norm. Be peculiar, be daring, and according to God's standards, be aware of your royal status, because your Father is the King of Kings. Don't be afraid to outwardly express what God has inwardly planted in you. Don't be a copycat of someone else, stop manufacturing synthetic ideas, and don't be a puppet to other people. No one should pull your strings. Know what you want and go for it. Exhale what God has inhaled inside of you. You are pregnant with possibilities! There are visions and dreams engrafted into your DNA, waiting to be discovered by you. Extract that information from within. Your life is supposed to be a reflection of God's glory. When people see you become who God has designed you to be, they should marvel at the beauty of God's glory being expressed through your authentic self. Let your passion be a driving force. When you truly discover your passion, it will definitely control you, and you'll be totally under its influence. You can't hide pregnancy. The baby bump grows every day, becoming bigger and more visible. Your behaviour and habits change to accommodate what is inside of you. Above all, avoid being pretentious in all your efforts; just be naturally you.

Live Life with Purpose, Know Your Mission, and Make a Contribution

All success begins when you become aware of your purpose and have a clear picture in your mind of precisely what you want in life. Jesus Christ knew what He was here on earth for. He knew who He was. Thus He made bold "I Am" statements: "I Am The Bread of Life (John 6:35), I Am The Good Shepherd (John 10:11), I Am The True Vine (John 15:1), I Am The Way, The Truth and The Life" (John 14:6). Who do you say you are? It is very important that you know who you are. Jesus' mission and purpose were embedded in what He called Himself. He knew His identity, mission, and purpose, and He would boldly declare it in what He called Himself, even amidst great opposition. Should I stop being who I am just because the next person feels intimidated by me? Definitely not! It's only the people who do not know who they are that get intimidated and jealous of you. Have a good self-esteem; believe in yourself and what you were meant to accomplish. Don't let other people's ill feelings and thoughts define who you are. Define yourself through God's eyes and boldly declare your identity. Be a man or woman of value, if you know what your value is.

As I said before, Jesus knew His purpose and mission, and He would boldly declare it. He knew that his final destination on earth was the Cross, but His eternal destination was rulership and dominion at the right side of the Father once He had conquered and fulfilled His mission here on earth. According to Luke 4:18, His mission was to reinstate the kingdom of God into the hearts of people. Thus His first announcement would be the arrival of the kingdom. (Matthew 14:17: "Repent, for the Kingdom of heaven is near.") His mission objectives would be to empower the people by preaching the gospel (good news) of the kingdom and deliver and heal the people. His purpose would be to die for the world, so that we would be reconciled to God, have eternal life through Him, and fully enjoy the benefits of the kingdom of heaven.

What is your calling? Is your calling to the lost in the world, or it's within the body of Christ? Know your station and where you belong within your call. What is your mission and purpose? Is your mission and purpose to encourage or empower people? Is it to support and help someone find their own vision and destiny? Are you living out your purpose? Are you making a contribution to society? What is your mission? Is your mission to demonstrate love in your community by giving to the needy and destitute? Do you have a clear picture in your mind of your destination? Pursue your purpose; fulfil your mission. It is your duty to find out what your purpose and mission are. Once discovered, don't be intimidated by what you have to accomplish. Do something about what you have to accomplish; don't die with purpose and vision buried inside of you. Be a world-class, ethical, and moral leader within your spheres of influence. Arise and make a difference in this world. Exude all that greatness that's within you. Make good use of your time before you expire. Leave a legacy behind. Also learn to diligently support and be profitable to other people's visions and businesses. The same favour will be returned to you when it's your turn.

When you cease to make a contribution, you begin to die.
—Eleanor Roosevelt

On the Journey to Destiny

Do what you feel in your heart to be right. For you will be criticised anyway. You'll be damned if you do, and damned if you don't.
—*Eleanor Roosevelt*

Instinct

Follow your instincts. Instinct is simply a natural innate impulse, inclination, or tendency. It's a natural aptitude or gift (i.e., the gift of making money). It is that inborn drive that makes you go to the left when others are turning right. It is that thing that makes you drop out of school and start a million-dollar business, because you have an idea and vision. (I'm not encouraging people to leave school here.) Instinct can be a great tool to self-discovery. The thing about instinct is that it's never taught in schools or any educational system. Education actually makes people rely more on what someone else has programmed or planted into their thinking pattern. Therefore people who rely more on what they have been taught through the education system become educationally rigid; some stop thinking for themselves. They are stuck in that box of education. Don't get me wrong; I'm not disputing education. All I'm saying is that people need to learn to listen to that voice inside that could give them the next breakthrough they so desire in life. Let not your thinking be limited to what the system has taught you! Use your imagination, follow your heart, but at the same time, take your brain with you. Now I understand why Einstein said, "The only thing that interferes with my learning is my education!" Learning begins when your thinking transcends the education system and when you start following your inborn drive. Learning starts when you go out into the practical world, meet real life situations, and implement life changing solutions, and sometimes you might have to think outside the book of what has been programmed into your brain through the education system when it comes to knowledge and application.

In following instinct, ask yourself what it is you do best without being taught how to do it. Some are born natural singers; they don't need to be taught how to sing. Some are gifted in planning events; nobody ever taught them how to. It is something that's innate to them. Some are born natural artists; nobody ever taught them how to paint. Listen to me: Greatness lies within each and every one of us. The only difference is that some act diligently upon what they are naturally good at. Be an expert in maximising your potential. Once you have found the treasure within, pursue it. And in pursuing it, get wisdom and understanding along the way.

The true sign of intelligence is not knowledge, but imagination.
—Albert Einstein

Born to Fly

In summary, when the mother eagle teaches her young ones to fly, she throws the eaglets out of the nest from a high cliff into the air. As they shriek in fear, father eagle flies out and catches them up on his back before they fall and brings them back to the cliff. This goes on for some time until they start flapping their wings. They get excited at this newfound knowledge that they can fly.

I believe that anyone can conquer fear by doing the things
he fears to do, provided he keeps doing them until he
gets a record of successful experience behind him.
—Eleanor Roosevelt

Flying can be intimidating and daunting at times. Just like the eaglets learning to fly, when you set your mind to pursue your dreams, goals and visions, and live life with purpose, the first few attempts to fly might not be as successful. But imagine God being the father eagle, carrying you on His back to take you right back to the starting point again for another try at flying. If not careful, you will have more reasons why you are not supposed to spread your wings and fly, than why you are supposed to. Instead of giving up at the first few or many attempts, I say, try, try, and try again until you eventually feel the wind carrying you beneath your wings. Then you will soon discover that flying is innate and has become effortless for you. If you are an eagle, the desire to fly is already inborn. You just need to learn how to do it; just be persistent in your attempts.

You will find out that when you begin to soar like an eagle, the ravens and ground-bound chickens will begin to notice you. It is a sad eagle that frets at the clucking noise of chickens, or the gurgling croak or harsh grating sounds of ravens! As an eagle, know your position and how majestic you are as the king of the air. Let the chickens and ravens make all the noise they like, but do not flinch, because you have the upper hand. Have sharp eyesight like the eagle you are, and stay acutely focused on your goal even when it seems afar off. When you keep sharp, acute focus, the obstacles will never be a distraction. Learn from the eagle and how it catches its prey. Let your flying altitude increase; never be stagnant. Flee complacency, it's a disease. Don't be too comfortable with where you are but desire to keep flying higher and higher.

Let the haters hate, but keep on keeping on and don't stop at nothing!

What Do You Feed On?

On your journey to authenticity, be careful what you feed yourself with. I've learnt that eagles do not feed on dead prey. They prefer fresh meat! If you are an eagle, stay current. Let your sources of information be current and up to date. Keep up with the times and don't get stuck in the old; at the same time maintain integrity and good ethical conduct. Be careful what you feed your mind with. What do you spend most of your time reading or watching? Does it help you move towards your destiny or achieve purpose? Does it build you up or destroy you? What are you watching? What are you reading? What takes up most of your time? What are you listening to? I leave that to your discretion. Feed on only the things that make you become a better person. Feed on the things that help you grow and become better in your area or areas of expertise. What you feed on will influence your behaviour and decision making processes. Be wise.

Choose the Right Company

Do not be so deceived and misled! Evil companionships
(communion, associations) corrupt and deprave
good manners and morals and character.
—Apostle Paul

When you are going somewhere, you can't just drag everybody along. Know who is for you and who is not for you, because everybody has got their own agenda. Who is your companion? Who are your friends? Who is the *best* friend? Whom is your heart knitted to, who are your connections? Whom is your soul tied to? Who are the people you have allowed into your circle? Networking is very important; it can be your defining point as an individual, and the wrong connections can later on prove catastrophic!

Show me who your friends are, and I'll tell you who you are.
—Dr Walter Masocha

If you are an eagle, you should learn to soar with other eagles and not with ravens or chickens, which are only ground bound and cannot fly! Surround yourself with people who are like-minded. This is an important point, because the people you entertain can influence your expedition to destiny. That's if you ever get there. They can influence either your escalation or your excavation. Your company can either make you or break you. Choose your companions and associates wisely. The people you entertain should bring out the best in you; they should help support your vision, dreams, goals, and purpose. Otherwise take austerity measures and choose who adds value to your life. Don't waste precious time with the wrong crew, because once time is lost, you can never reclaim it. It is better to be alone than in the company of fools. You find that the less you associate with some people, the more your life will improve.

> *He who walks [as a companion] with wise men is*
> *wise, but he who associates with [self-confident] fools*
> *is [a fool himself and] shall smart for it.*
> —King Solomon

People can only go as far as their thoughts allow, and also the company they keep around them, because the company you entertain, can influence your thinking and behaviour. Your company can either stimulate expansion of positive thinking or diminish it with negativity. If the people around you have no vision, if they are not going anywhere in life, then I say steer clear of such. Otherwise you might eventually end up in the same predicament with them, unless you are the one to enlighten them and put vision and purpose back into their lives if they are willing to listen and change. The people that you become close and intimate with affect the very essence of your being; they affect your soul. When you associate with someone, there is more of a spiritual connection, and you tie yourself to that person (or people). You'll notice that you are more likely to develop similar character traits with the people you spend time with. Choose to associate with quality, with the best, and become even better. Be wary of unhealthy soul-ties; loose and undo ties that bind. Remove the clatter in your environment and purge your soul. Don't sabotage your own future and destiny by making the wrong decisions when it comes to company. Also, don't hold on to stale relationships; good relationships are fruitful and mutually beneficial! If they are no longer fruitful, then it's time to move on. Be friendly with everyone but intimate with only a few, and the few must be the best.

In life we are given people for a reason, a season, and for life!
—Dr Walter Masocha

Know which category your friends, associates, and acquaintances fall under. They are either for a reason, for a season, or for life. Don't hold on to unfruitful unions; know when it's time to move on and do it gracefully.

The Confidant

Through it all, have a confidant. Ecclesiastes 4:9 says, "Two are better than one; because they have a good reward for their labour. For if they fall, the one will lift up his fellow: but woe to him that is alone when he falleth; for he hath not another to lift him up." The dictionary defines a confidant as one with whom you can share a private matter or secret, trusting them not to repeat it to others. It describes this person as a "bosom friend," and your bosom is your chest area, the cavity that houses your heart. This person is a person at heart. You are not afraid to trust that person with your heart, because they have got your back and your interests at heart. That person can be your soul mate, buddy, close friend, brother, adviser, mentor, or pal. Whoever they are, they are highly trusted and a valuable asset to be treasured and cherished. You can lean on them in times of trouble. When you fall, they are there to lift you up. They are a pillar of strength and support and are like-minded with yourself. They stick up for you, stand up for you, and never to betray you, come what may. Their loyalty is indisputable! Again, choose wisely!

Environment

It is important to understand that, when God created man (Genesis 1, 2), He first created man's ideal environment, which he could thrive in first. After He had created man's environment, He created man to dwell in that environment. He made sure that everything man needed to be fruitful and multiple was in that environment. This makes us understand why it is important to be in the right environment, because a product trying to function out of its manufacturer's ideal environment will not thrive! Take fish out of water, and it will die. Put man to dwell in water, and he drowns. God is principled, and He does not break His own rules (manufacturer's instructions). Make sure your environment makes you flourish as an authentic person. God had to move Abraham away from his place of birth to a place God showed him, so that he could flourish and become all that God designed him to be in that place (from Ur to Canaan). The same applies to us. If our environment is not conducive for fruitfulness, it is best we move somewhere where we can truly flourish. Don't get stuck in a supressing and suffocating environment. Do something about it and never allow your gift or soul to be stifled.

Business-Wise

What's your authentic brand? Learn to brand yourself to create a lasting impression on people. What is it that makes people more interested in you? Be marketable within moral bounds. Remember the three things that matter in business: product, service and marketing. If you grasp the concept behind these three points, you will develop skills to successfully expose and maximise your authentic brand. How good is your product? Is it marketable? Do you provide quality services marked with a touch of excellence? When it comes to marketing, do you have an effective strategy? Have business savvy! Create jobs for others to succeed in their areas of expertise whilst enhancing and profiting your authentic brand. Connect with the best of the best, to get the best out of the best.

Also in business, employ and surround yourself with people who support and are profitable to your vision. The people you employ have the same effect as the type of company your keep around. What type of people are managing you or your business? Management in the wrong hands will cost you! Be wise; the wrong employees can be the downfall to your vision or business. Associate with the right business partners; employ diligent thinkers, who also have vision and goals of their own. Be wary of those who just want to make money and have no love for, or passion for the post they apply for. Employ the people who have the passion and are enthusiastic about their responsibilities, especially those who are like-minded and have the same spirit of succeeding as yourself. When something goes wrong in the business, the blame is on you and not them, because you employed the wrong people and allowed them to handle your affairs. Pick your employees wisely and have a discerning heart. Qualifications are good, but experience is better because your knowledge goes beyond the qualification. Don't just go for the qualified, but go for the determined, because determination (positive attitude) will take you where qualification cannot. The problem with the qualified is that they only know and stick to what they attained during their studies. Their thinking is limited to what they have been taught, unless they are the sort to break beyond the limits of academics. But the diligent dreamers thinks beyond the qualification. They see possibilities all around; they break the rules and help take you where no one else has gone before. They are thought leaders who stimulate progress and expansion, they possess the power of imagination, and they have the right attitude. Attitude matters more than qualification.

Cross Networking

*If you want to go fast, go alone, if you want
to go far, take others with you!*
—African Proverb

Avoid monolithic networking or connections if you are ever going to reach your maximum potential. Learn to cross-network. If you are a musician, don't just network with musicians, but learn to network also with the physician, the lawyer, the hairdresser, the car racer, the scientist, the wedding planner, the chef, and the pilot. Don't just stick with people within your area of expertise, because, I believe, it stunts growth as an individual. Cross networking will help you spread your wings wider and in turn help bring out other gifts and interests you never thought you had. I know of a friend who is a gifted singer, an amazing chef, and a successful wedding planner. If he had only stuck to singing and never kept an open mind, he would have never discovered all these other hidden talents. Add as many colours as you can to your palette, and make the journey interestingly vibrant. When it comes to connections, associates, and acquaintances, you need diverse perspectives of influence and contributions on your table. Keep an open mind; you will be surprised what other gifts are inborn to you; and just come naturally as you cross network.

Have Character and Be Graceful

Character is doing what is right when nobody's looking.
—J. C. Watts

Above all, have character and be full of integrity and good moral ethics. Let your character be outstanding and graceful. Let love, joy, peace, long-suffering, gentleness, goodness, faith, meekness, and temperance define your character. How perfect will it be if your life is characterised by the Word of God. Now that is my desire. Charisma can take you to the top indeed, but only character will keep you at the top. Look at the qualities Jesus Himself possessed. He was full of wisdom, knowledge, and understanding. The Bible says He grew in wisdom and in stature. In what direction are you yourself growing in? Think of what it is that makes you up? What is it that defines your character? What message do you send across about yourself to other people? Have good character and conduct. Whether in the presence of people or alone, learn to be consistent.

Be poised and of a gentle spirit. Be principled (have a set of rules that you adhere to), practise temperance (moderation, self-control, and self-restraint). Proverbs 25:28 says, "Whoever has no rule over his own spirit is like a city broken down, without walls." If you are a city without walls, there is no form of protection or defence, no control of who enters and who goes out. In ancient times, cities were fortified with strong walls as a way of defence and protection. With such security, it was hard for the enemy to penetrate such a wall. A city without walls was easy to attack. Anybody would enter the city at will and do as they please. Don't be like a city without walls! Otherwise your enemies will come in and plunder all the treasure hidden inside your soul. Beware of the wolves that come in sheep's clothing, pretending to be your friends, and yet inside they are wolves ready to destroy all the good you have inside. They whisper into your ear and cause you to bring down your defences, giving them advantage over your soul. Resist such character assassins; flee the urge to conform to peer pressure. Stay principled, because principles are what you set for yourself as a wall of defence against life's enemies. Don't let someone else cause you to break or bend them. Let assertiveness be the guard to your walls.

Be graceful, elegant, stylish, tasteful, refined, dignified, distinguished, discerning, cultured, cultivated, polished, dashing, opulent, grand, and exquisite. Don't be afraid to let the treasure in you manifest for the whole world to see. Contribute something good to this life, and do it with style and grace, maintaining good character and integrity, even when no one is watching you. Who is the real you, when nobody is around? Think about that!

Self-Esteem

The strongest factor for success is self-esteem; believing you can do it, believing you deserve it, believing you will get it.
—Zig Ziglar

You can never become all that you are meant to be if you suffer from a low self-esteem. Confidence can take you right to the king's dining table. Confidence has the power to take you places you've always admired in your head. Confidence is that extra spark that makes you stand out more and display your beautiful colours in front of a crowd. Always walk tall and keep your head up. Have the mentality of the royal person you are. Some people have had a pretty rough upbringing, which has affected how they see themselves. If you are one of them, you need guidance and counselling, and I hope this book proves beneficial. It all goes back to your thoughts. Read the principle about thoughts and deliver yourself. Seek counselling and surround yourself again with the right company, with people who make you better. Having the right self-esteem is important. You are not fully authentic if you have a negative self-esteem. Believe in yourself even when no one else does, develop a thick skin, and fill your mind with positive thoughts. Have the "Yes I can" attitude. As long as you can tell yourself "Yes I can", or "Yes I will", and believe it in your heart, then you will. The "Yes I can" mentality is a major confidence and self-esteem booster. Telling yourself "Yes I can" when opportunity presents itself will help you tackle what seems impossible. It broadens your perspective and opens your mind to ideas that can be the solution to tackling what seems to be an unconquerable mountain standing in front of you. Telling your mind "Yes I can" or "Yes I will" enlightens your spirit and lifts up hope. You become hopeful where hope was lost. Your faith is strengthened as long as you keep on believing. The "Yes I can" mentality is the attitude improver. It steers your attitude in the right direction, leading you to light if you were trapped in a dark tunnel. Have a great self-esteem; be bold and confident. Never look down upon yourself or sell yourself short. Have a strong, positive self-image; it is preparation for success. In all your confidence, remember not to be arrogant, pompous, or proud! Big-headed people are a pain to be around, especially those who try and belittle others. Keep a cool head and never be a braggart! Be humble. Remember; it's not what others say about you that defeats purpose in you, it's what you say about yourself that threatens your destiny. Speak into your life what you want to see yourself become!

Credibility

Honesty is a very expensive gift. Do not expect it from cheap people.
—Warren Buffet

Being authentic requires a high level of credibility. Are you believable? Simply put, credibility has to do with being worthy of belief or being trusted, of being convincing, and of being a person of your word. When you give your word, do you keep it and do as promised? Are you an honest, reliable, and valid surety for someone? Never make a promise if you can't keep it. It is better not to say anything than to make an empty promise. It only makes you less reliable and less trustworthy.

Faithfulness: With credibility comes faithfulness. How loyal are you? How loyal are you to your partners (not only in marriage but also in business)? How loyal are you to your friends and family? How loyal are you to yourself, with your dreams, plans, and ideas? The qualities of faithfulness are fidelity, loyalty, constancy, devotion, trueness, true-heartedness, dedication, commitment, allegiance, adherence, dependability, reliability, strictness, exactness, precision, and authenticity! When you have a vision, are you consistent in following it through? When promise to commit to something, do you follow through your promise to the end. Are you faithful enough to be trusted with something of great value? Are you faithful with time keeping? Are you faithful with church attendance? Are you faithful with your gym routine? How far do you measure up the thermometer of faithfulness. Check your credibility level! Ask yourself how people around you perceive you. Will they be able to vouch for your faithfulness? Authenticity requires a great deal of faithfulness, faithfulness to self and faithfulness to others!

Accountability

When you are accountable, you are responsible, liable, and answerable. Most of the times, people tend to dodge from owning up to their actions.

There is always something or someone to blame, and yet if we only learn how to simply accept our actions and take responsibility for them, we will be able to progress in life. If you are accountable, you are an honourable person – morally correct, honest, ethical, principled, righteous, right-minded, noble, full of integrity, illustrious, distinguished, eminent, admirable, and worthy of every bit of respect. Accountable and credible people are easy to work with and prove profitable. When things go wrong in your plans, learn to take responsibility, identify the cause of the problem, and adjust accordingly. You find that when you are responsible, people will take you more seriously and respect you. Take responsibility for your actions. More people would learn from their mistakes if they weren't too busy denying them.

Take the Best of Yourself and Make It Better
The only person you need to compare yourself to is who you have been.
The only person you need to be better than is who you are now.

Stop whining about past mistakes, missed opportunities, or qualities about yourself that you are not pleased with. When you make a mistake, get up and get back in line. Proverbs 24:16 says, "A righteous/just man falls seven times, but he gets back up again." What makes him righteous is the fact that he has enough sense to realise his mistakes, learn from them, and move on. You cannot be an overcomer unless if you go through complications, even humiliation, failure, disappointment, hurt, discouragement, you name it. The reason why most fail is they never make the decision to get up again and get so discouraged that they remain on the ground. Self-pity is not an admirable quality in someone who wants success. When you have a pity party, I liken it to someone chopping the roots of their own tree of success with a sharp axe. If this is you, my question is, How long have you been chopping, and how much have you already chopped off? Eventually that tree will fall and become good for nothing. Do not dwell in self-pity land, move house! Instead of focusing on the things that you do wrong, why not start appreciating those things you do perfectly. Here is a challenge: Go and buy a jotter and write down the things that you are really good at. Every day focus on improving yourself in such areas and write down your progress. As you take the best of yourself and make it better, also do your utmost best to bring out the best in others. Commend others on their strongest and shinning attributes and be the one to push someone else to greatness! This takes me to my next point.

Reflection

Taking time out to reflect can prove beneficial. At the end of the each day, take some time to just reflect. Spend some quiet time alone in silence and reflect on everything that has happened during the day. Evaluate yourself, and note the areas that you could improve and better yourself as an authentic person. List down every blessing, read the Word, meditate, and say a prayer of thanksgiving. Spend some time meditating on God's Word, because that is the most healthy and nutritious food for your soul and spirit. When you read and believe His Word, it gives you motivation and courage to face the next day. Meditate and let His Word transform you each and every day until your life epitomises the Word. When your life epitomises the Word, your authentic self is enhanced. It's like applying wax to a car to make is shine. You are the car, and His Word is the wax. Prayer is the fuel that drives your engine and propels it towards destiny.

In a Nutshell

Dream Big and Think Big

You will always gravitate toward that which you secretly most love.
Into your hands will be placed the exact results of your own thoughts!
—James Allen

Do not limit yourself because of your current environment or because of people around you. Do not let people drag your boat under water. Sometimes you might have to disassociate yourself with boat sinkers! Get rid of the excess baggage. If they do not add value to your life or propel you towards destiny, loose the bonds. If you believe yourself to be an eagle, know that you are meant to sore high above everybody else. Limit your time with negative people. They are like poison; they pollute your environment and clog your vision. Don't die with purpose hidden inside of you. The worst tragedy in life is not death; the worst tragedy in life is letting purpose die within you and taking it into the grave with you. Denounce the spirit of abortion of purpose and vision. Don't abort the greatness that's within you; don't abort the life you envision and are supposed to have. Also don't be around vision aborters, and again I reiterate, stay away from negative people. They are like weeds that stunt growth and choke up destiny. Eliminate such!

Eagles do not flock. Don't be afraid to stand out of the crowd, because you were not meant to fit in but to stand out! Do not be intimidated with your own uniqueness. Why should you hide it? They might call you weird and all sorts, but who cares? Understand that they are not going where you are going! Dream big, think big, think outside the box, and be the one who creates the box! Most of us are stuck in boxes that others have created. Be a trailblazer and a trendsetter. Trailblazers are always coming up with new inventions and ideas. They set the trend. They do things that have never been done before or attempted by anyone. Sometimes they might be labelled "controversial" by the small-minded, boxed-type-of-thinking people, but trailblazers won't let anything or anyone stand in their way. Be a trailblazer; set the trend! Look at Jesus. He was controversial in His day, but now His legacy is celebrated all over the world by millions of people. He has become the centrepiece of Christianity. We could learn a great deal from Him about being authentic.

Dream big, have a vision, live with purpose, know what your purpose is in life and pursue it, know your mission and fulfil it. I ask again, What are you meant to accomplish? What do you desire to do? Flee small-minded type of thinking and think bigger because you serve a big God, a God who owns the universe and has no limits or boundaries. Don't let negative people control the way you think or the way you perceive life. Become everything that God has ordained you to be from the beginning. Allow Him alone to lead, because once He takes the lead. Then the right people will come into your life and help you achieve your vision. Never feel limited and never limit yourself. They say the sky is the limit, but I say there are no limits at all except the ones we create in our minds. Don't cripple yourself by thinking that you are too young or too old, or don't have the right qualifications (because there are many qualified but are not living to their maximum potential). It is not how and where you start that matters; it is how you finish. Better is the end of a thing than its beginning. Just like you stir sugar in a cup of tea, stir the gift inside of you. Don't let it lie dormant, but let it be active! Let it add sweetness to life, giving you something to look forward to everyday. Don't let the gift die; God gave it to you for a reason. Start now and have the right attitude, because your attitude determines whether you sore high like an eagle or struggle to accomplish anything at all. I like what Solomon says in Ecclesiastes 9:11 "Time and chance happens to everyone", whether you think yourself intelligent or not, whether you were born less privileged or into aristocracy, whether you are disabled or in good health. We all get the same 24-hour day, breathe the same air, and busk in the same sun. What we do with the time and chance that we are given in this life depends on our willingness to just live life and excel, having the right frame of mind and a positive attitude towards life altogether.

Ecclesiastes 9:11
New King James Version (NKJV)

I returned and saw under the sun that—
The race is not to the swift,
Nor the battle to the strong,
Nor bread to the wise,
Nor riches to men of understanding,
Nor favor to men of skill;
But time and chance happen to them all.

*God can renew your strength and revitalise your energy. You're
never too old or too young to accomplish your dream.*
—T. D. Jakes

The Crown (Genesis 37 - 50)

Joseph was a dreamer, his brothers envied him because of the nature of
his dreams, and because their father loved him the most. The dreams
Joseph had, revealed his future greatness; he would be a prince/ruler
over his family, and over a nation. This pricked his brothers and caused
them to be jealous! No matter how jealousy they were, this did not stop
God's plans from coming to pass (when God says yes, no one can say no.
When He has set you up for a blessing, no one and nothing can stand
in your way). His dreams eventually came to pass many years after he
had been thrown into a pit, sold into slavery, falsely accused and thrown
in prison for a crime he did not commit. The journey to destiny for
Joseph was a tough and rough one, but through it all, he maintained
his integrity, he did not lose character, he remained principled and
persevered through the rough times. He did not lose hope, or faith in
His God, he trusted Him and held on to the promise. Wherever he was
(even in prison), he prospered, and everybody loved him! (When you
have God in you, everything falls into place in your favour, no matter
the environment you are placed in). It is these qualities that Joseph had,
that made him rise to power and become a ruler over a great nation
during those times. Joseph was wise in his dealings, and left a legacy
that we now read of in The Great Book, and has been read of for over
thousands of years! I'm sure you get the jist and moral of the story. The
road to success is never easy, it's always bumpy and rough, but he who
endures to the end will receive the crown. Be constant and persistent
in purpose!

Power Notes

➢ Don't be afraid to be different and stand out.

➢ Know who you are, because you are the best you could ever be.

➢ Excavate the hidden treasure deep inside and reveal the glory.

➢ Know your mission and purpose.

➢ Define yourself. What does God say about you? What do you call yourself?

➢ Don't be afraid to fly. Flying is only meant for the brave and risk-takers.

➢ Have vision. A man without vision is as good as dead.

➢ Learn to cross-network. Expand your colour pallet as an artist of your own life.

➢ Have good character and be principled. Don't be like a city without walls.

➢ Be graceful, full of poise and elegance.

➢ Choose the right company, because the company you keep can either make you or break you. They are like a compass, pointing you in either a good direction or a bad direction.

➢ Don't feed on old information; always be up to date and current. Eagles do not feed on dead things!

➢ Have a positive self-esteem. Maintain a positive attitude.

➢ Take the best of yourself and make it better.

➢ Be credible, be accountable, and be faithful.

➢ Reflect. Time alone in silence can prove beneficial.

➢ Think big and dream big. There are no barriers. The only barriers we face are created in our minds. Learn the art of flying.

➢ Do everything with an extra special touch of excellence, and the world will marvel at and admire your work.

Purpose in your heart to lead an authentic lifestyle!

Principle #12:

BE DILIGENT, DON'T PROCRASTINATE

The hand of the diligent will rule;
but the lazy man will be put to forced labour.
—King Solomon

Stop with the Excuses

"How long will you sleep, O sluggard? When will you arise out of your sleep?" *(Proverbs 6:9)*. Laziness is a disease that stifles productivity. In this principle I will show you the characteristics of a diligent person, compared to that of a lazy person. Infact, every attribute of a diligent person which I will reveal, is the exact opposite when it comes to a lazy person. Lazy people are masters of inactivity, they are qualified in doing nothing. They oversleep until they are tired from sleeping. They procrastinate, and generally waste time indulging in unfruitfulness. Sometimes they are actually great thinkers and very intelligent, but do nothing with their ideas. They are always the sort of people you have to give a push in order for them to move. They love doing things the last minute, at a furious pace, trying to compensate for lost time. Most of the times, they are very proud. You cannot correct them, or instruct them wisely because they will take offense. They are wise in their own sight, big headed, and never reasonable *(Proverbs 26:16)*. They are not aware of what season it is at any given time, in other words; they are the sought who do the right things at the wrong time, and the wrong things at the right time, and the end result is no achievement. They seem busy at times, but busy doing the wrong things. It's better to be busy doing the right things, at the right time, and producing the right results. The bible even says that "He who does not work, neither should he eat" *(2Thessalonians 3:10)*. "Yet a little sleep, a little slumber, a little folding of the hands to sleep: So shall your poverty come upon you like a vagabond, and your want like an armed man." *(Proverbs 6:10-11)*. Get off your back and work; become; produce, and use your God given abilities and skills to become what God has destined you to be. True success comes by when we learn to utilize what God has naturally given each and every one of us, and yet nothing just happens whilst you are sitting and doing nothing.

On the other hand, the diligent show care and consciousness of their work and duties. They are industrious, hardworking, particular, meticulous, rigorous, thorough, attentive, careful, heedful, earnest, constant, persistent, dedicated, committed, driven, active, busy, unflagging, untiring, and tireless. Diligent people never make excuses; they make an effort despite difficulties of the task. They are always willing and ready to learn, even if it's something out of their comfort zone. Excuses cripple people, because so many could be far ahead in life if only they had stopped with the excuses. If you can't see your way out of something, don't make an excuse but create a way out! The diligent person is quick to get up, and get back in line when they fall. They keep on trying until they get something right. They never use a handicap as an excuse. They have the "Yes I can" mentality.

Look at the people whom God used in the Bible. Moses was stutterer who delivered a great nation out of bondage. Rahab was a prostitute who bore the lineage of Christ. Jacob was a deceiver who gave birth to the nation Israel. Jeremiah and Timothy were "too young", but God used both for His glory. Abraham was in his old age. Peter denied Christ but later on repented, and on this rock Christ built His Church. Elijah was suicidal at some point. David had an affair and committed murder, and yet God still called him "the man after His own heart"(1Samuel 13:14). Jonah ran away from God, but God used him to deliver and save a whole city after he repented. Zacchaeus, even though short, never used his height as an excuse not to see Jesus. He diligently sought a way out and climbed a sycamore tree! What's your excuse then? When it comes to the things of God, avail yourself, and let God use the skills He has invested in you. God is after a willing and available heart, because no one is perfect except Him. Avail yourself to God and be profitable to His kingdom and to His people. Also be profitable to your own family and everybody around you. The diligent are always available; that's the dependability factor!

The Diligent Rule

According to the words of wisdom by King Solomon, the diligent are the ones who rule. They strive to be efficient; they do everything on time and in time. The diligent have got impeccable organisational skills. They are always the first ones to arrive for a meeting. They don't waste time, because they understand the value of time. They always plan ahead. They are always the first to come up with ideas and suggestions; they don't back away. They are the first ones to make contributions and are usually quick to respond when given a task. They are easy to work with and always daring.

When faced with a challenge, the diligent are the ones to rise up to the challenge, face it, and provide a way out for others to follow. The diligent make good leaders. When they have a business plan or an idea, they are quick to implement it. They never sit on their hands. They are always innovative and creative, because their brain is always active thinking of ideas. They somehow seem to possess boundless energy, always seeking opportunities, creating opportunities, and seizing the moment. Procrastination is never their master. They are always in the forefront, and the lazy feel intimidated by them. When they have an itch for something, they scratch for it. They are go-getters! Indeed the diligent bear rule! They are self-motivated and do well without supervision. You trust them to get the job done efficiently.

It is one thing to itch for something, and yet quite another to scratch for it.
—Dr Walter Masocha

Go the extra mile: The diligent always have the right attitude and mentality. They have an astounding work ethic, and their hands are always busy being productive. They go the extra mile, and they do it with a willing heart and positive attitude. In life you will find that if you do more than what you are paid for, eventually you will be paid more than what you do. Go the extra mile in the way you love and care for others, go the extra mile in the way you give, go the extra mile in the way you exhort and encourage others, and go the extra mile in your prayer life. Be diligent in every aspect pertaining to life. Go the extra mile in rendering your services to others, and do it with gladness of heart. Life always gives back what you put into it.

Occupy: People who are diligent are always occupied, because they are busy being productive. They don't waste time, even in their occupation. They are organised and always seem to be ahead of everything and everyone. There is a common saying that goes like this: "The devil makes work for idle hands!" Never allow yourself to be idle; otherwise you become the devil's playground. Keeping yourself occupied is always a good distraction from unhealthy thoughts. If you keep the young people occupied by giving them something exciting to do, you help them stay out of trouble. Be innovative, full of creative ideas and inventions that positively impact the trajectory of humanity. Let your thinking capacity expand and your intellect be sharpened. Pursue the things that stimulate fruitfulness and productivity in your life.

> *While 9 a.m. to 5 p.m. and what happens between*
> *that time is important, what happens from 5 p.m. to*
> *9 a.m. off the job is infinitely more important.*
> —Zig Ziglar

What do you spend your time doing after working hours, or after school or lectures? Is it a time for you to indulge in unproductive activities or a time for you to look for ways to better your life? Are those so-called free hours spent being productive, or they are spent doing nothing at all?

Be knowledgeable: Get wisdom, get understanding! The diligent take the time to educate themselves. They don't sit on their brain or wait to be spoon-fed. They read books; they research; they take down notes. Remember, knowledge is power, and wisdom is applied knowledge. Study to show yourself approved. Do not perish because of lack of knowledge. Get knowledge and seek revelation! Your greatest enemy is ignorance. What you don't know might kill you.

Ecclesiastes 7:12
New King James Version (NKJV)

For wisdom is a defence as money is a defence,
but the excellence of knowledge is that wisdom
gives life to those who have it.

The diligent rule, they are always in control!
—David Conellias

Purpose in your heart to be diligent, and never to procrastinate!

Principle #13:

BE A GOOD LEADER

A good subordinate always makes a good leader.
—Dr Walter Masocha

Leadership takes skill, effort, and a whole lot of patience. Everybody is a leader in some way, but then there are those who stand out to lead others. Now you cannot be a good leader if you can't lead yourself first, let alone lead yourself in the right direction. Always respect the people above you and be a blessing to them, because one day you will have people beneath you. Remember what I said about the law of reciprocity? What goes around comes back around! A good subordinate always makes a good leader. Leadership is not only in business or religious organisations but also in families or schools. Leadership comes at different levels in life, and whatever the setting, as a good leader you always need to be equipped. When you are fully equipped as leader, you are better able to equip others in turn. They say practise makes perfect; learn to perfect your leadership skills every day. When good leaders fall and make a mistake, they always rise up and learn from their mistakes, and then make corrections and move forward. Remember, time will not wait for you. So there's no time for pity-partying!

A leader loved is a leader fully respected. As a leader, earn the respect of the people you are leading. Don't earn their fear. This also goes for fathers in the homes. A good father is loved and respected. Instilling fear in your children will only make them resent you and fear you but not love and respect you sincerely. Below are a few leadership empowerment notes I have drafted up, just to equip the leading leader out there. Dare to be an authentic leader par excellence!

Leadership Empowerment

> ➢ A good leader is loved and respected by the people, not feared! You can make people fear you, and they will; but they will never respect you.

> ➢ A good leader always solves the problem. They are not the problem themselves. They do not place blame on others. They never point the finger at someone else. If anything goes wrong; they take responsibility of the problem and fix the breakdown. They never make a decision without judgement.

> ➢ A good leader is sympathetic and empathetic. They are genuinely concerned about the welfare of others, and help as much as they can.

> ➢ A leader must be transparent and honest.

> ➢ As a leader, don't be naive; know whom to trust and whom not to.

> ➢ A good leader always encourages, exhorts, and builds others up. They are not a destructive force! In business, you build people, and then people build the business. The equipped subordinates help establish the business!

> ➢ A good leader generates enthusiasm; they say "we", and not "I". There is no "I" in team. Leaders always incorporate and value the input of their subordinates and followers.

> ➢ Good leaders listen to the opinion of others and try to incorporate them were appropriate. They are not hush and brush. They are wise in their dealings. When a leader lacks wisdom, the ship he or she is in charge of will eventually go down. The Bible says in James 1:5; "if anyone lacks wisdom, let them ask from God who gives it generously to all, without finding fault." And also Psalm 111:10 says; "The reverential fear of the Lord is the beginning of all wisdom!"

> ➢ A good leader remains calm even under immense pressure. When the storm is wrecking the ship, the good leader keeps the crew and passengers calm by reassuring them.

- A good leader leads by example. They lead. They don't just know how it's done, but they show how it is done. They always take the first initiative and never back down from challenge.
- A good leader depends on goodwill and not authority.
- Good leaders ask; they don't demand! They are polite and respectful of others. If you want respect as a leader, then learn to respect others as well.
- Leader treat others the way they themselves would want to be treated, with respect.
- Good leaders give credit. They always compliment on other people's achievements without selfishness and they do not take credit of other people's achievements. People love to be praised; it boosts their confidence and self-esteem. You should always be aware of that as a leader. Learn to give praise were praise is due. Be generous and genuinely heartfelt with your compliments, and people will love you even more.
- Good leaders are never jealous when others do better than them. They are proud of other people's achievements and will even encourage further.
- Good leaders gracefully accept when they are wrong and are willing to change.
- A great leader is a great leaner. Great leaders learn from others, too. They are not arrogant or puffed up. They are not too proud to ask for help. Humility marks true leadership. Humble yourself, and you will be lifted up. The one who is proud and exalts himself will soon come tumbling down. Better to be humble than to be humiliated.
- Good leaders fight for, defend, and protect the people they lead, their vision, or the vision they are under. They never expose the weaknesses of the establishment they are under.
- As leader, make it a point to know your subordinates very well. Make an effort to remember each individual's name and to call them by their name appropriately. Put an effort into learning to pronounce even the most difficult of names. You will find that your subordinates will love you and appreciate you for the

effort. Everybody loves the sound of their name. So make it a point to remember names. Come up with a strategy that will help you to remember people's names.

➤ Good leaders do not easily give up or make excuses. They show commitment and are long-suffering!

➤ When the ship is drowning, good leaders will drown with the ship. They don't jump ship and leave the crew and passengers to perish.

➤ Leadership is not dictatorship. You do not impose on people but pay attention to their needs, give a solution to their problem, and lead the way out.

➤ As a leader must be genuine and sincere. Otherwise the people you lead might eventually lose interest in your leadership. Learn to genuinely smile at people, let the smile come from the heart, and let the people you lead feel the warmth emanating from you. It's the little things sometimes that make people appreciate and love you. You will get their full support and loyalty in paying attention to such simple detail.

➤ A good leader must be meek, gentle, kind, welcoming, and genuinely loving. Meekness is not weakness but strength under control.

➤ Good leaders show maturity and have good character and conduct. They are accountable, credible, believable, and dependable. They uphold good moral ethics.

➤ A good leader has vision. A good leader is principled and follows protocol. A good leader is focused and disciplined.

➤ A good leader is always optimistic, always looking at the positive side of matters. They are resilient, tough, strong, and adaptable. They bounce back quickly when hit.

➤ A good leader must possess good management skills. Be it time management, money management, crisis management, mind management, or resource management.

➤ A good leader is always diligent! Diligence marks true leadership, along with accountability, faithfulness credibility, obedience, and submission to those above them.

- A good, successful leader has a successor.
- Great leaders possess servanthood! They serve God and others with zeal and passion! How well do you serve God? How well do you serve your family? How well do you serve your community? A true leader offers their service for the benefit of others. Their aim is to be profitable.
- In conclusion, be strong, but not rude. Be Kind, but not weak. Be bold, but not a bully. Be humble, but not timid. Be proud, but not arrogant.

Matthew 23:11–12
New King James Version (NKJV)

But he who is greatest among you shall be your servant.
And whoever exalts himself will be humbled, and
he who humbles himself will be exalted.

Some of these points may apply to you, and some may not. Most of them are general. Try and apply as much as you can and improve your leadership skills. Good leaders take the time and effort to educate themselves. Don't be complacent. Be constantly looking for ways and strategies to better yourself as a leader.

Purpose in your heart to be a good leader!

Principle #14:

LEARN MANAGEMENT SKILLS

Failing to plan is planning to fail.
—Dr Walter Masocha

The purpose of learning management skills is to improve efficiency and productivity, achieving fruitfulness in all areas of life. The topic on management skills is quite broad and diverse, but I've just listed a few basic skills which I think apply to everyone in general and are not particularly directed towards a certain area.

Planning and Preparation

A big shout out to Kyle and Tiffany Bynoe for teaching me about the "five *P*s" of success: *Proper planning prevents poor performance.* If you fail to plan, you plan to fail. Planning shows organisational skills as an individual. The outcome of your overall performance in life, and on a daily basis, will be based on how much you prepare and plan for anything. Start by learning to plan your day when you wake up. Make a note of everything you have to do during the day and tick as you go along. You find that you become efficient and productive, and the day is not wasted. In your planning, don't be rigid. Make leeway for changes to the plan, because anything can come up and change the course of the day. Planning also includes simple things like making a grocery list of the things you need to buy in the house before you go to the supermarket. If you plan what you are going to buy, you not only save finances but you also save time. Proper planning and preparation are key for success! Your performance in life can only go as far as your level of preparation, and the results always prove that. Always learn to plan and to prepare, be it for a music show, a job interview, or a recital. Whatever it is, plan and thoroughly prepare for it in advance for an excellent outcome.

Time Management

Lack of direction, not lack of time is the problem. We all have 24 hour days.
—Zig Ziglar

Time is the true measure and currency of life. How you spend it determines the quality of your life, you become whatever you buy with your time. Everything and everyone around are vying for your time. Time is important because your time is your life. The key to effective use of time is prioritising. Time is very precious. Once lost, it can't be reclaimed back, and that's a part of your life that falls into history with every second past. Learn to manage your time well. Learn the art of prioritising events as the day goes by. When your priorities are set in order, you preserve and protect your life, and progress is guaranteed as far as purpose and goals are concerned. Prioritising right shows discipline and guarantees success. Avoid wasting time and energy, chasing after insignificant things or worrying over insignificant issues and people. Don't be busy with the wrong things. In fact don't just be busy and in your busyness unproductive. If your priorities are right, you become effective or fruitful. King Solomon understood time and seasons and wrote a whole chapter in the Bible about that (Ecclesiastes 3). Doing the right thing at the wrong time can produce negative results. For everything there is a time and a season, and one ought to be aware of that in order for priorities to be set aright. In your execution and use of time, don't count the things that you do but do the things that count! Have direction; know where you are going and what you want to achieve; be orderly and well organised.

Start the day by doing the things that are most important first, and make the least important last on your list. This proves beneficial if you have an important deadline to meet, or important meetings and interviews. Avoid being late for meetings or appointments; learn to always be on time. Timekeeping is important whenever there's an agreed time limit. Always strive to adhere to that; it shows accountability. Learn reverse planning; this is when you start by jotting down/planning where you want to be first (the end first), and what you want to achieve at different points in time, then work backwards listing every step that you need to take to get there, until you come to the point where you want to begin the process. When it comes to your time; always plan things way in advance to avoid doing things the last minute. Reverse planning can help you keep with time and avoid being late. Each activity has to be carried out within its allocated time frame; otherwise everything else falls behind.

Fig. 1.1

Item (Process of setting up PA system)	Reverse-planning times
PA system to be ready	17:30
Test PA system	16:30 – 17:30
Set up equipment	13:30 – 16:30
Unload equipment	13:00 – 13:30
Transport equipment	10:00 – 13:00
Load equipment	09:00 – 10:00
Bath, breakfast, pray	06:30 – 09:00

Note: If items are not done at the correct time, either another later item will need to be sacrificed or things will happen late. Carrying out reverse planning will allow activities to be done by the correct time.

Finance Management

Budgeting

Budgeting is basically making sure that you are spending less than what you are bringing in, and planning for both the short and long-term. It is simply a program of spending wisely, or you can call it a 'personal financial plan.' It's a proactive approach rather than a reactive approach to managing your money. Budgeting makes it easier for people with incomes and expenses of all sizes to make conscious decisions about how they would prefer to allocate their money. Is your spending within your means or it's superfluous? What are the things that you spend your money on; ask yourself if they are necessity or just a luxury? Beware of impulse buying. Nothing wrong with being luxurious if you have the means to do so, but at the same time, spend your money wisely. Avoid the temptation to overspend. Watch out for little trinkets and little gadgets, they are meant to attract your eye so that you spend. Beware of sales, sales, sales, they lure you into spending more than necessary under the camouflage of 'sale'. When it comes to saving money, there's quite a lot you need to keep your eye out on. Always have an emergency back-up plan in place, in case the unexpected happen. Be wise with your spending, and have business savvy and financial acumen (*astuteness, awareness, sharpness, cleverness, sharp-wittedness, brightness, smartness, common sense, insight, intuitiveness, enterprise, flair, power of reasoning, savvy, know-how*). Your budget should evolve as your circumstances change, it should cater for times when you have more coming in, and the times you have less coming in as well.

The secret to creating wealth is knowing the difference between your "*Assets*" and "*Liabilities.*" Assets are not only things you *own*, but are rather the things that pay you, or bring you more income (*cash-flow*). These should increase as you progress in life and generate you more revenue (*money, cash-flow*). Liabilities on the other hand, are the things that *cost* you money. For example a car, you own it, yes, but it costs you money to run and maintain it. You have to constantly fuel it up, take it for service, pay MOT for it, pay road tax for it regularly, and get it insured. When it breaks down, it costs you money to get it fixed. Now that's a liability. Same applies to a house, it is an asset when it pays you money, but also a liability when it costs you money (mortgage, costs of maintaining it/*upkeep,* bills).

Now, a "*broke*" person's mentality is to spend spend spend without creating more cash flow. The "*broke*" person *wastes* money on unnecessary "*things*" or "*stuff*". You give them money, but it's like their pockets contain *holes,* the first thing they will think of is spending the money, not saving it, or rather investing the money. They are the sort who end up having *more month at the end of the money*! If you want wealth, then cut out your liabilities, and increase your assets! Educate yourself on how to create wealth and make passive income (income received on a regular basis with little effort required to maintain it). Lack of education in this area can cost you! Solomon said in the book of Proverbs; "*In all thy getting, get wisdom, get understanding!*" Don't spend the profits you make, but rather use them to acquire even more assets that will generate you more income (even passive income), that's how the "*rich*" people make more money. Don't *appear* to be rich by spending superfluously so that you impress, but rather let your pocket speak for itself genuinely. Don't get yourself into a trap either, trying to make "*quick money,*" riches and wealth don't accumulate overnight, it's a process whereby one has to be patient, and consistent in application of wisdom and knowledge. That's one of the main keys to success, it doesn't happen overnight, but it is progressive. Play your cards right, and be smart.

Budget Plan

Below I have drafted a simple and straight forward budget plan to follow. Drafting a plan doesn't have to be complicated, it's usually the execution of the plan that's a challenge if one is not disciplined. Budgeting requires discipline and temperance is one of the fruit of the Spirit. But remember, if you can put your mind to it, then you can achieve it. Apply cost management skills; it is simply a process of planning and controlling your budget so that you don't overspend. Have a good money saving strategy. Take austerity measures when it comes to spending. If you find that taking the bus to work saves you more money than driving to work, then adjust accordingly. On your personal budget, eliminate what is not a necessity and be principled when it comes to spending. Always write down your expenses and purchases to keep an eye on what you spend the most on.

Fig. 1.2

Total income per month: £650

Item	Cost
Tithe	£65
Investments	£20
Phone	£20
Fuel	£40
Food	£50
Insurance	£30
Clothes	£50
Rent/mortgage	£100
Council tax	£50
Heat and gas	£40
Other expenses	£50
Savings	£100
Total expenditure	**£615**

Balance at the end of the month: £35

This table is meant as guide only, and the figures might not be as realistic, but it serves the purpose. Notice that when you learn to budget your finances and stick to your budget plan, chances are, you'll be left with more than enough to either add to your savings or to spend responsibly. Just because you have excess money left, does not give you the licence to squander it all. Save, save, save, and don't waste. One day the excess money will come in handy.

Tithing and Giving

The tithe might leave your hand, but it will never leave your life!
—Dr Walter Masocha

Just like we pay taxes to our earthly governments, a citizen of the kingdom of heaven pays tithe to the heavenly government. By so doing, we build ourselves treasures in heaven, where no moth or rust can destroy them, and we obviously unlock the benefits of the kingdom attached to the tithe. The Bible is clear in that the tithe belongs to God. A tithe is a tenth of your increase (substance). Nowadays it mainly equates to income received from various sources. In the Bible, tithe could be anything that was considered as substance (money, crops, livestock, material possessions, spoils from war, etc.) There was no limit to what you could tithe to God. In your planning, always remember tithing. Now we move to the spiritual aspect of finances. Tithing and giving open financial "portals" in your life. It is another key that gives you access to God's endless supply. A portal is simply a doorway, gate, or entrance, especially a large imposing one. I like that term *imposing one*, because when something is imposing it is impressive, striking, arresting, eye-catching, dramatic, spectacular, stunning, awe-inspiring, remarkable, formidable, grand, majestic, lofty, and splendid! And all these terms refer to the blessing of God connected to the tithe! Remember when Malachi says, "And you will be a delightful land", it confirms the imposing nature of the opened window (portal) of heaven. All nations will see how blessed you are. It's a blessing that everyone sees before their eyes and marvel at the doing of the Lord in your life.

Malachi 3:10–12
Amplified Bible (AMP)

Bring all the tithes (the whole tenth of your income) into the storehouse, that there may be food in My house, and prove Me now by it, says the Lord of hosts, if I will not open the windows of heaven for you and pour you out a blessing, that there shall not be room enough to receive it. And I will rebuke the devourer [insects and plagues] for your sakes and he shall not destroy the fruits of your ground, neither shall your vine drop its fruit before the time in the field, says the Lord of hosts. And all nations shall call you happy and blessed, for you shall be a land of delight, says the Lord of hosts.

Abraham understood the concept of tithe. In Genesis 14, after conquering Chedorlaomer and the kings who were with him, Abraham met Melchizedek, the king of Salem (king of righteousness and peace, who was the high priest and a type of Christ resembling the Son of God; Hebrews 7:1–4). He offered a tenth of all the spoil he had collected from the defeated kings. Melchizedek blessed Abraham in his office as high priest. Abraham's faithfulness caused God to respond. After all these things had happened, the next chapter tells us of the promise God made with Abram. His tithe unlocked God's promise to him and his descendants, and indeed he was truly blessed, he and his household. When we choose to trust God with our finances and possessions, He will trust us with His limitless resources. God is not a robber. He is never after your money, because He doesn't really need it if you think of it. What God is after is the blessing that accounts to you. When you tithe, you keep portals of the blessing open. You find God begins to open windows of opportunity for you. He begins to bless you with million-dollar business ideas. He begins to give you intellectual breakthrough were access was denied. He doesn't just give you money back but a way to make the money, a way to generate income. Only the diligent will reap the full benefits of tithing and giving. A lazy person will not see the benefits of tithing. They will think tithing is not working for them, and yet they'll be sitting on gold and not know it! Get up and start thinking! Be a hard worker, open your eyes, and create opportunities, because your tithe has opened the door. Your tithe activates the blessing into your life. When you have the blessing, favour is on your side. You find favour with God and with men. You find favour in your education. You even find favour in your business dealings! Your tithe also wards off the enemy. Your money is like a defence against the enemy, and God even confirmed it when He commanded us to bring all the tithe into His storehouse. By so doing, "He would rebuke the devourer for our sakes." (Malachi 3:10-12) Now think of everything that the devourer has stolen from you, and start fighting back with your money through tithing and giving.

Proverbs 10:22
King James Version (KJV)

The blessing of the LORD, it maketh rich, and he addeth no sorrow with it.

Never Withhold

Never withhold from God. Withholding only constricts the portals of heaven and sabotages your own breakthrough. The Bible says being stingy or parsimonious only leads to more poverty. It is only the generous soul that is made richer (Proverbs 11:24-25). Another Scripture says if you sow sparingly and grudgingly, you will reap sparingly and grudgingly. If you sow generously though, you will also reap generously (2Corinthians 9:6). These principles not only apply to tithing but to giving in general. Look at Abraham our father. He was blessed because he did not withhold from God his one and only son Isaac. This is a prophetic lesson to be learnt.

Genesis 22:15–17
New King James Version (NKJV)

Then the Angel of the LORD called to Abraham a second time out of heaven, and said: "By Myself I have sworn, says the LORD, because you

have done this thing, and have not withheld your son, your only son
— blessing I will bless you, and multiplying I will multiply your
descendants as the stars of the heaven and as the sand which is on the
seashore; and your descendants shall possess the gate of their enemies.

Abraham was blessed and multiplied in possessions because he trusted in the provision of God more than in what he already had access to. (Jehovah Jireh!) Look at the blessing he got simply because he did not withhold from God. Sometimes giving has to be sacrificial in order to get the breakthrough you desire. When it's a sacrifice, it's something you value, cherish, and hold dear. It might be the very last penny in your bank account or your last meal (like that of the widow of Zarephath); it might be that one thing you have between life and death, and yet you trust God to intervene and give you something even better in return. Just like He did with the widow of Zarephath (1 Kings 17:7–6). The Word says that after she had sacrificed her last meal to the prophet in obedience, God gave a word through the prophet Elijah, reassuring her that the bin of flour was never going to be used up, and the jar of oil was never going to run dry, until the day the LORD would send rain on the earth. She and her household ate for many days! Giving unlocks the miraculous.

Trust in the Lord with all your heart and lean not on your own understanding when it comes to matters of giving. I encourage you to give whenever the opportunity presents itself. Be generous and hearty when you do it. Don't be selective. Spread your seed "across the field", for you do not know where the breakthrough is going to come from. Do not just wait for opportunities to give to arise, but go out and seek the opportunities yourself.

Ecclesiastes 11:6
New King James Version (NKJV)

In the morning sow your seed,
And in the evening do not withhold your hand;
For you do not know which will prosper,

Either this or that,
Or whether both alike will be good.

Activity: *I want you to clench your fist and the open it. Clench (close) it again and then open it widely. The same is a reflection of what happens in the spirit realm. A clenched parsimonious fist (with regards to withholding from God), is an indirect command that you are passing to have the portals of heaven shut against you! Open it in the act of giving generously, and you command the portals to be opened. What's your attitude when it comes to giving to God and others? God generously rewards the one who does it cheerfully, heartily, and willingly. This is a law in motion, whether you are a Christian or not.*

Money Matters

The Bible says, "Money answereth all things" (Ecclesiastes 10:19), and so it does. We all need money to survive and get by in life. Money is simply a form of exchange, and without it, our access to some of this world's necessities is limited. Money is a form of power which everybody works hard to gain, and the Bible says the love of it, is the beginning of all evil (1 Timothy 6:10). That's why power is abused by many. People want to be in control of the quality of life they desire to have. As I have mentioned before, the more you hold on to money (in greed, selfishness, and stinginess), the more you will lose it, and the less you will have. The more liberal and generous you are with it, the more access is given to you in the natural and in the supernatural. You allow more room to be made available to receive even more in abundance, as long as you have the right attitude towards money. Your money is actually a weapon against the enemy, and the enemy knows that! That's why he would blind people from participating in the house of God and the building of His kingdom. That's why he tries so hard to create more reasons for us to be selfish with it and struggle to part with it. Your money can be the answer to the breakthrough you are looking for, if released as a seed of faith! Learn to sow that seed for whatever breakthrough you might be believing God for, because your money offered to God, and in the service of generosity towards others, will eventually answer for you when breakthrough is needed.

Prosperity

"For I know the plans I have for you," declares the Lord, "plans to prosper you and not to harm you, plans to give you hope *and a* future.*"*
—Prophet Jeremiah

Some interpret Jeremiah 29:11 as the Lord having thoughts (which are plans still), of peace and not evil. When the Lord blesses you with His peace and lifts up His countenance towards you, believe me, that is prosperity already. For how can you have good success without peace? The Bible clearly reveals that giving is a major key to prosperity, along with reading the Word and obedience, to complete the full blessing. It is the key that can make us unlock the plans God has for us to prosper. Prosperity (the blessing) is not only in terms of finances. I liken prosperity in its totality to a scrumptious cake of eight big slices that you can enjoy along with everyone else connected to you (family, friends, and associates). Look at Abraham. Wherever he went he prospered. Even the land and people around him (like Lot) prospered and became fruitful, because they were around a blessed man. Finances is one of the slice to this cake, and so is wealth and the strength to get it (wealth can be ideas, inventions, wisdom, knowledge, and valuable possessions, which may include property, cars and any material thing), and then good health (emotionally, physically, psychologically, mentally, and spiritually), protection, favour (both with God and with men as well as breakthrough), joy, love, and peace. All these are the benefits of prosperity that come from the Lord through giving to God, others, and the needy, and through obedience and acting upon His Word.

The Bible says in the book of Job that when we give to the poor, we will never lack bread on our tables. God desires for us to take care of the poor, the widow, and the needy. He says whatever we do to the least of these, we have done also to Him. That's why the richest people in the world are always giving to charity. God honours that, and He honours His law of giving and receiving. The key to financial breakthrough is not withholding what you have but giving it away. When you give it away, it goes and multiplies, bearing much fruit to your own account. God rejoices when His own children prosper. The Bible says that His desire is that we may prosper and be in good health.

People who have the gift of giving somehow seem to know how to generate the money as well. See, when you are a giver, God makes channels available for you to prosper. When it comes to attaining wealth, one must learn the fruit of patience. Be consistent in applying the law of giving; don't be discouraged when you see things not happening in a "flash". True wealth is birthed out of a patient heart. It took me seven years to acquire the first automobile of my dreams, which was a great lesson for me. Never rush when it comes to success, because in trying to get a "quick fix", you might lock yourself up in a prison. Follow the proper ethically sound and godly channels.

Note: The Bible says the lazy hand will be made poor! If you want riches and wealth to come your way, then being lazy will not help you get there. Only the hard-working will reap the benefits of their labour.

Borrowing

*If you buy things you do not need, soon you
will have to sell what you need.*
—Warren Buffet

The Bible says we are to lend to many nations and never to borrow when we have the blessing. Avoid unnecessary borrowing, especially if you do not have the money to repay it; it only leads to debt if not careful. When you borrow, you are a *slave* to the one who is loaning to you. Borrowing comes in many forms, and the obvious examples are mobile phone contracts, long-term or short-term loans, and any other form of contract that requires you pay back some money into it.

Payday loans: Payday loans are never a permanent fix to your financial problems. In fact, if you miss payments, they might become a permanent problem instead. Avoid payday loans. Most of them charge a ridiculous APR (interest) on payback, and the more you delay in paying the loan back in full, the more interest you get charged. As long as this interest keeps building up, you are getting yourself deeper into debt. Don't dig holes into your financial bag. When in debt, you do not need another loan to pay off an existing debt; if you get one, you keep on exacerbating your financial situation by going further into debt. Instead of getting another loan, you can get another job, or find other means to make more money.

Long-term loans: Only take a long-term loan if you have the financial means to pay it back without it being a hassle. The principle about loans is still the same.

Overdrafts: These are to be avoided unless necessary. The bank charges interest every time your account is overdrawn, and it is happy to make more money from you, which it will unless you have what is called a planned overdraft. A planned overdraft is meant as a fallback plan in case of unforeseen financial circumstances. However, there is still a charge for any form of overdraft, especially if you delay bringing your account back to balance. Some banks, however, only charge a fixed amount for an agreed-upon overdraft limit.

Debt management: If you find yourself in debt, start prioritising where to spend the money in your budget. When you prioritise your outgoings, you create more change to pay off your debts as quickly as you can. Cancel the things you don't need from your budget, and keep them out of it until debt is paid off. There are also some debt consolidation companies that are willing to help without extortionately charging you for their services. Some can even do it for free; all they do is help you pay off your debt (or debts) by consolidating them into one lump sum which you can pay off monthly until the debt is cleared. Again, choose which company to use wisely. Make sure you read the clauses before you sign any agreement, because in most cases, the catch is in the clause, and if you don't read the small print, you might get yourself entangled in a trap. Make that decision today to be absolutely debt-free, owning no one – no bank, no business, no loaning institution – a single dime! Look for ways to be debt free; either get a second job, or establish an income generating business to attain more revenue.

Investing and Saving

Investing: Working hard is good, but we should also work smart. Investing is a good way of making profit by putting your money into some form of financial scheme, shares, or property. This is another area in which you need wisdom and guidance, or *financial acumen*. Weigh the pros and cons before you invest in any particular scheme. Take your time studying the activity of your chosen scheme, and don't be too hasty. This is money we are talking about; the wrong move can cost you all your investment. As Warren Buffet says, "Don't put all your eggs into one basket". Spread out your investments; don't focus on one scheme only, in case that particular egg breaks. If you had five to begin with, then you will at least have four left to profit from. Investing is all about taking a risk, but *never test the depth of a river with both feet!* Always have a fallback plan; have money saved up in case things don't go the way you wish them to. Buy stocks and shares that keep increasing in value, buy rental properties that people pay to live in. Real estate and stock shares are the most common form of passive income. Work smart!

1 Thessalonians 4:11–12
Amplified Bible (AMP)

To make it your ambition and definitely endeavour to
live quietly and peacefully, to mind your own affairs,
and to work with your hands, as we charged you,
So that you may bear yourselves becomingly and be
correct and honourable and command the respect of the outside world,
being dependent on nobody [self-supporting] and having need of nothing.

Investing has to do not only with joining existing schemes but with generating income by setting up your own business schemes as well. Have an entrepreneurial spirit, be innovative, be creative, and start something which you can call your own. Use your God-given skills to your advantage. This is when authenticity can work to your advantage in creating wealth. What are the things that you are naturally good at? Is it making wedding cakes? Is fixing cars part of your authentic code? Start making money with the things that you are good at. Also note that wherever there's a need or a demand, there's opportunity to make money. Never have only one source of income; make investments to create a backup. Look for other ways to generate income, and have financial acumen.

Savings

Savings are a good way to create riches. When you have money saved up, you are richer than one who doesn't have anything saved up at all. With saving comes discipline. Resist the temptation to touch your savings unnecessarily, or else your savings scheme will be in vain. There are different savings schemes which I shall list for your benefit. I'm mainly going to refer to the UK savings system; please find out what options are available in your country.

1. **Cash ISAs** *(Individual Savings Account):* These allow you to earn tax-free interest. UK taxpayers usually pay tax on interest earned from savings in line with usual rates – so there's usually a 20 to 40 per cent loss upon return. ISAs are a sensible place to start when looking for a home for your savings. Cash ISAs do not always offer the most attractive interest rates on the market, but their tax-free status means they can provide savers with better returns than standard savings accounts. However, there's a limit to how much you can put in your ISA; once you've reached the limit, you will need to move to another type of saving. To find the best rate, compare the gross (pre-tax) interest rate offered

on a cash Isa with the net (after 20 per cent tax) rate you would receive from a standard savings account.

2. ***Instant-access savings accounts:*** These do exactly as their name suggests. They allow you to withdraw your money quickly and easily. Emergency savings should be put in an instant-access account. Some accounts come with a plastic card that can be used to take out money from cash machines, some offer over-the-counter withdrawals, and many allow online bank transfer out of your account, penalty free.

3. ***Notice savings accounts:*** These work differently than instant access accounts. Instead of having quick access to your money when it suits you, you have to tell your provider in advance that you want to make a withdrawal. If you make an emergency withdrawal from such an account, you are likely to lose interest. You should keep an eye on the interest rates, because these accounts are likely to come with variable interest rates, and you might need to switch to a more competitive deal.

4. ***Regular savings accounts:*** These require you to deposit money each month without fail. Thus, they are ideal for savers who are just starting out and want to save in a disciplined way. These may limit the number of withdrawals you can make in a year, and this means you cannot use such an account for emergency savings. It is also likely to restrict you from investing more than a certain sum each year, preventing you from placing extra cash into your account as and when it suits you. Again look at the interest rates, and weigh your options. Check to see whether the interest rate is fixed or variable.

5. ***Fixed-rate bonds:*** These offer a fixed interest rate on your cash for a set period of time. While they often come with a higher interest rate than instant access, notice, or regular savings accounts, opening one means giving up your money during

the term of bond. These terms can extend over a period of one to five years. The longer you are prepared to lock your money away, the higher your return will be. Use this type of account only if you are confident that you won't need to use the money before the term is out, since making an emergency withdrawal can land you a hefty interest penalty. Investing in this type of bond protects your savings returns in an era of falling rates, but the opposite is also true.

Weigh your options with savings accounts. Always check to see whether interest rates are variable or fixed. If you find a more competitive deal, it's worthwhile transferring your money. Always keep an open eye on your investments. Be diligent in your dealings. Learn how to generate, manage, and distribute wealth in a wise manner.

Resource Management

Be a good steward of your possessions! If you want more to come your way, then start by being faithful with the little that you have. God will only entrust you with bigger assets once you learn to manage the little ones that you have. Stop wasting the resources that are made available to you, and learn to maximise them wisely. Again, I bring back the terms *savvy* and *acumen* (which mean more or less the same thing). I've noticed that the opening of doors in our lives is progressive. Each level of access you gain requires that you remain constant in integrity and following your principles (if you have any) with regards to resources you have access to. Each level of access also brings a slightly higher degree of responsibility. Have skills that will make you cope and manage well at every level of success you reach in life.

When carrying out either personal projects or business projects, never over-allocate your resources to one project. Let there be an equal distribution of resources so that you maintain balance and get even returns from all angles of your projects. Managing resources requires wisdom and diligence. Never employ someone to manage your resources who has no clue what they are doing. We have a perfect example in Joseph. Leading up to the famine in Egypt, God gave him wisdom and favour regarding how to handle the resources Egypt had during the seven years of plenty before the famine began. Joseph was able to interpret Pharaoh's prophetic dream about the famine that was about to hit the whole of Egypt and the surrounding land (See Genesis 41). Because of the spirit of wisdom upon Joseph from God, he was able to quickly come up with a wise strategy to help deliver Egypt from a seven-year famine.

Genesis 41:33–36

New King James Version (NKJV)

"Now therefore, let Pharaoh select a discerning and wise man, and set him over the land of Egypt. Let Pharaoh do this, and let him appoint officers over the land, to collect one-fifth of the produce of the land of Egypt in the seven plentiful years. And let them gather all the food of those good years that are coming, and store up grain under the authority of Pharaoh, and let them keep food in the cities. Then that food shall be as a reserve for the land for the seven years of famine which shall be in the land of Egypt, that the land may not perish during the famine"

Joseph and Wealth Management

Joseph was only thirty years old when he gave this wise advice to Pharaoh. That set him in favour with the king, and he was made ruler over the people of Egypt, for there was no one else found to be as wise as he was. Pharaoh and his people followed the advice of Joseph and collected one-fifth of the produce of the land during the seven years of plenty. I promise you, if no one like Joseph had risen during those times to give such advice on resource management with regards to grain, surely the land would have perished. In chapter 47 of Genesis, Joseph is elevated to Governor, and we further see Joseph's wisdom in managing resources when the famine became even more severe and people had run out of grain. Joseph still had reserves of his own which he began to sell to the people and, in turn, gain more wealth. He was clever. Whilst everybody was busy spending, Joseph was saving up; the people would come to him and offer their livestock in exchange for grain. The evidence of Joseph's managerial wisdom is laid bare in chapter 47: he always had a strategy. Even when Egypt had run out of money, Joseph never ran out of a plan which would generate more wealth for him and for Pharaoh. When others were spending, he was receiving more stock and resources that would enable him to make more from what he had.

Resource management takes wisdom and discipline. When you have that, you will find that whilst others are going through "the recession" and scrounging for pennies, it might be the perfect opportunity for you to make more money by making use of resources available to you. When others are going through a recession, God can even give you a business idea that will prosper you and make you the one to lend help to others, and in turn to gather even more resources and wealth to your benefit. The times when there is "plenty in the land" are the times to gather as much as you can. It's not the time to spend frivolously but rather the time to stock up and save. You will find that when the famine comes, whilst others have nothing, you will have plenty and even be in a position to make more wealth as long as you remain constant in wisely managing what is accessible to you.

Solomon and Wealth Management

Another perfect example of resource management would be Solomon. Now the Bible's account records that there was no man or king wealthier than he, even up to now. How could that be? He asked for wisdom, and God gave it to him; therefore he was able to deal wisely in most of his business as leader of a great nation. Every year, Solomon would receive twenty-five tons of gold, amongst other things. He had a vast array of resources and wealth accessible to him (read 2 Chronicles 9:13–29). Such great wealth can only be obtained by a wise person who has astounding resource management skills. His wealth came from commerce and trading (1 Kings 9:26–28), gifts (2 Chronicles 9:1, 9 and

1 Kings 10:25), tribute money from other countries who acknowledged his superiority (1 Kings 4:24), heavy taxation (1 Kings 12:4), and his inheritance from his father David. Solomon was so rich that even all his cups were made of gold; none were made from silver. The good thing about Solomon is, he shared his God-attained wisdom through the books of Proverbs and Ecclesiastes. Read the books. The question I pose is this: What is your management strategy? Have a strategy that works well and profits you well in the end. When God has blessed you, your strategy prospers.

Other Management Skills

Crisis management: How well do you cope under pressure? When faced with a crisis, it's time to rise to the challenge and show leadership/managerial skills. What's your strategy in all of this? Crisis management can be applied even in events management. Organising events takes skill, effort, patience, organisational skills, proper planning and research, working with the right people, and delegating duties accordingly. You have to be able to deal with the level of pressure that comes with the job, at the same time maintaining excellence. Always have a fall back plan, if plan A doesn't work, what's plan B then? As much as we can be people of faith, and believe in the supernatural, it's quite inevitable that the unexpected always happens when you least expect it. It's the organised and strategic thinker that comes out a winner in the midst of chaos. You have to learn to adapt to any situation expeditiously, do not be intransigent either! Mix your faith with practicality, because we do live in a natural and practical world after all.

Mind management: This takes us right back to the principle on thoughts! Align your thoughts aright! Put a filter on them, choosing what to accept and what not to accept. Accept only the healthy thoughts that enhance your life. Think well of others, too; avoid ill thoughts. Let your mind be fortified and resolute. Think of ideas and inventions that positively impact the trajectory of humanity.

Change management: As I said before, a little change is good. Don't be rigid. If something is not producing positive or fruitful results, then I say it's time for change. Learn to take and manage change well. Change is beneficial to growth; where there is no change, the chances are that growth is stunted! Learn to be flexible. It makes life easy for you.

Purpose in your heart to master good management
skills, and to be organised!

Principle #15:

THE LAW OF RECIPROCITY

Be not deceived; God is not mocked: for whatsoever
a man soweth, that shall he also reap.
—Apostle Paul

Reciprocity is one of the laws set in motion by God, just like the law of gravity – that what goes up is eventually pulled down by the force of gravity. Another law is seed time and harvest time: when you sow, you reap what you sow. The law of reciprocity is like the boomerang effect of life. What you do to and for others will in turn be done to you. It's a law in motion which is fixed just like the law of gravity.

Be careful how you treat others, because the same will be done to you; that's life. If you want to be loved more, then give out plenty of love. If you want to be respected and celebrated, then respect and celebrate others. If you want to be appreciated, then I say you start by appreciating and complimenting others. The things you do for others always come back to you, good measured, pressed down, shaken together, and running over. Your success in life is also rooted in how you help others succeed. Successful people always seek opportunities to help others succeed, but unsuccessful people always ask what's in it for them. When you are stingy, you get less and less in life, but the more generous you are, the more you get. Jesus made reference to this when He talked about giving:

Give, and it will be given to you: good measure, pressed down, shaken
together, and running over will be put into your bosom. For with
the same measure that you use, it will be measured back to you.

—Jesus Christ

The quality of what you receive is determined solely by you! When you give the best, you receive the best. When you give average, then you also receive average. That's why Paul said not to be deceived, for what a man sows, that he will reap. If you sow seeds of corruption, then corruption will be returned to you. I call it the law of attraction; you attract what is in you, and what you give out in life. You attract the same kind of people as yourself. If you don't like what you have been receiving, or the type of people you have been attracting, then check what is in you, how you have been treating others, and how you have been giving! As you can see, giving is not only a matter of donating money but is mainly what you do for others, and what you do *to* them. If you give of your time, then when your turn comes for help, someone will take time to do the same to you as well. You are the one who is in charge. You determine the quality of your own life by the type of seeds you sow through your actions to others. He who refreshes others will in turn be refreshed.

And as you would like and desire that men
would do to you, do exactly so to them.
—Jesus Christ

So instead of wondering why things are the way they are in life, or why people treat you the way they do, take inventory and see where you fall short. The solution to life lies within you. Every action will give birth to re-action, and it can either be negative or positive. You attract what you celebrate, and you repel what you resent.

Purpose in your heart to always do good to
others, for you receive what you give!

Principle #16:

BASICS

Mind Your Own Business

1 Thessalonians 4:11
New King James Version (NKJV)

*That you also aspire to lead a quiet life, to mind your own business,
and to work with your own hands, as we commanded you*

Yes, mind your own business and know whom to share your business with. A lot of conflict and unnecessary stress can be prevented if we learn to mind our own business and pursue peace with all men. Most of the times, some people are busy trying to fix the next person, or poking their nose into matters that do not concern them. I believe the only time you can mind someone else's business is when someone actually asks you to do so, or when someone asks for your help or opinion. Other than that, keep your nose in your own business. You will find that you'll be at peace. If you want peace, never give your opinion to other people unless they ask for it. You can seriously save yourself the trouble. Learn the art of silence, opening your mouth with wisdom only when you are expected to. Never give people a piece of your mind. You might be left with no peace in the end.

Share your business only with a confidant, someone whom you sincerely trust and can open up to. Many people had their lives and dreams messed up because they confided in the wrong people. Again I say; don't be naive. Know whom to trust. Information in the wrong hands can prove disastrous. Be wise whom you open your mouth to. Not everyone is truly your friend, and not everyone is on your side. Have that discerning eye, and let discretion be your guide.

Avoid Arguments:

Never argue with a fool, onlookers might not be able to tell the difference.
—Mark Twain

Avoid arguments and walk away from the opportunity to argue. Maintain your elegant nature and always be poised. The one who refuses to argue and maintains meekness always has the upper hand. Avoid giving answers that might spark an argument. Don't let the flame blow up by giving a response that aggravates the situation. Remember the Bible says in Proverbs 15, "A soft or gentle answer turns wrath away." Always be the bigger person and refuse to come down to the level of the person who wants to argue. Maintain your dignity and that royal priesthood you possess. Whenever the opportunity presents itself for you to argue, always remind yourself that you are royalty and should act like one. Be a peacemaker, for blessed are the peacemakers. They shall be called sons of the King (God). Sometimes silence is the best solution when faced with opposition and confrontation. Beware of the things that try and take away your peace. The bottom line is, be of a gentle spirit.

Ecclesiastes 7:9
Amplified Bible (AMP)

Do not be quick in spirit to be angry or vexed, for anger and vexation lodge in the bosom of fools.

Stop the Blame Game

A man can fail many times, but he isn't a failure until he begins to blame somebody else.
—John Burroughs

Pointing fingers at others is the lowest of lows. Refrain from it. Learn to take responsibility for your own actions, and learn to own your mistakes. Repeat the previous principle about accountability! I like what one person said: "When you point a finger at someone, you have three other fingers from the same hand pointing back at you." Resist the urge to blame it on someone or something. When you blame others, you give up your power to change. Even go as far as covering up for other people. Instead of getting the joys of getting someone into trouble, be selfless and cover the sins of your brother. It is the bravest who takes the blame upon themselves. Refuse to be a sell-out. Be honourable, and at the same time use your brain! Do not blame anyone in your life. Good people give you happiness, bad people give you experience, the worst people give you a lesson, and the best people give you lasting memories that leave footprints in your heart.

Never Judge; You Are Not Perfect Either

The least amount of judging we can do, the better off we are.
—Michael J. Fox

We all know the famous quote "He who is without sin, let him cast the first stone". Jesus said that to the mob that surrounded the woman who was caught in adultery. They were all ready to stone the woman to death because she had committed a sin and violated the Abrahamic law. I always asked the question, Where was the man she was caught with? I don't think she committed the sin by herself. However coming to my point of judging, Jesus made it clear that we should not judge others, because we all have sinned and fallen short of His glory. The Bible even says that the same measure we use to judge others will be used against us. How do you perceive other people? Are you the one who is quick to find fault and make up a conclusion about someone based on your preconceived notions? Every time I'm tempted to prematurely judge someone, I always remind myself that I am not God.

The Bible says only God is perfect and no one else. If God is the only perfect one, then my position in all of this is quite clear. I am not God, neither will I ever fill His shoes. Let God alone be the judge, because I also need His grace and mercy. Learn not to judge. Be welcoming to people and give others a second chance, just like God did with you. I like the quote that says, "Judging a person does not define who they are, it only defines who you are". The faults you *supposedly* see in others are the same faults that are in you. You only notice what you yourself harbour inside. In other words, when you judge others, you are only judging yourself! That's why the Bible tells us to stop looking at the "speck" in our brother's eye, when we ourselves have a "plank" in our own eye to deal with. Deal with your own plank first before you try and remove the next person's speck. Stop fault-finding as if there's a reward for it. It's only a waste of your precious energy. Instead of focusing on the heap of dirt on a budding rose, why not focus on the glory of the beautiful flower instead.

Do Not Criticise

Criticism, like rain, should be gentle enough to nourish
a man's growth without destroying his roots.
—Frank A. Clark

Refrain from negatively criticising. People who often criticize and find fault are the ones who are not doing anything better with themselves anyway. It's usually the unproductive people who have time to sit down and negatively criticise other people's efforts and hard work. Do not find fault, but find a remedy instead. Instead of criticising, why not air your views in a polite manner without making someone feel belittled. Positive criticism is good, but in your criticism don't leave the other person feeling small or belittled. Do it with respect for the next person and be polite. Don't make their ideas and efforts seem useless. Otherwise they will not take your critique or advice. Make sure you leave the person with their ego still intact. Like the quote says, your criticism should be gentle enough to nourish a man's growth without destroying his roots.

When your criticism destroys other people's vision, you have killed these people, unless they've got thick skin to bounce back. Gentleness, respect, politeness, and wisdom are key. Your criticism must be constructive and not destructive.

Gossip

Small minds discuss people, average minds discuss events, and great minds discuss ideas.
—Eleanor Roosevelt

Steer clear of gossip. It only reveals your small-minded nature! Instead of gossiping, use that energy to discuss ideas that can better your life or somebody else's. Gossipers are the greatest liars. You find that most gossip is twisted truth, and in most cases its intention is to defame someone else's character. When you have a personal grievance with someone, why not go to them in private to try and iron out the issue without an unnecessary audience. Go and make reform with the offender or offended, with an intention of winning each other back and not destroying each other. This is simple and healing practice and yet ignored. You find that gossipers are manipulative, bitter most of the times, and selfish. They cause a lot of division among people. Gossipers have got a serpentine spirit and evil intentions most of the times. They are baptised in pride and arrogance. Deceit is their master, and the fruits of their evil work always show. Refuse to accept gossip. When opportunity for gossip arises, turn away from it and refrain from being defiled. When you accept gossip, you have allowed your mind to be corrupted, it is better not to have anyone to talk to than to be surrounded by gossipers. Graduate from small-minded thinking and start discussing ideas that are constructive. It is only the small mind that has got nothing to do, that wastes its time discussing other people's business. Gossipers are also the greatest fault-finders! Resist the urge to entertain such. Don't be in the habit of uncovering your brother's or sister's nakedness (their shortfalls, weaknesses, mistakes, or sins) to the world, but be the one to cover them when you see them naked. In so doing, God will reward you with the same courtesy and kindness. How would you feel if someone was to strip you naked (deface) in front of other people? Remember, you reap what you sow!

A lot of problems in the world would disappear if we talk to each other, instead of talking about each other!

Principle #17:

ETIQUETTE

Manners easily and rapidly mature into morals.
—Horace Mann

According to Wikipedia, etiquette is a code of behaviour that delineates expectations for social behaviour according to contemporary conventional norms within a society, social class, or group. It has all to do with being courteous, polite, well-mannered, gentlemanly, ladylike, genteel, cultivated, gracious, kind, considerate, pleasant, proper, discreet, thoughtful, diplomatic, and basically having the right morals. How do you treat others? Are you considerate? Do you know when to speak, or do you just speak out of turn? In a so-called free world, many (especially the younger generation) have lost their morals and become rebellious. They have forgotten the value of humanity and simple good morals, which brings and keeps people together in a peaceful environment. Their passions do not conform to the dictates of reason and justice.

Apologise: Learn to apologise when late for meetings, appointments, or any form of gathering with an agreed time. When you want to take a trip to the lavatory during a meeting or during a lecture, excuse yourself gracefully and make your way out quietly without disrupting others. Also, when you can't attend a meeting for whatever reason, common courtesy is to notify whoever is in charge and apologise out of politeness and respect.

Coming to personal matters, saying "I'm sorry" when you have wronged someone can be hard for the proud and arrogant, but it gives you peace of mind, especially when it's sincere and from the heart. Learn to say "I am sorry", and mean it. Realise your mistakes and repent for them.

Apologise even when you respond late to a message, an email, or an announcement that requires your attention. Show some politeness in this aspect.

Respect: Treat yourself and others with respect, and in return, you get respect back as well. Respect everybody in general, be it your family, friends or co-workers. Be courteous and considerate. Learn to respect your elders and the elderly as well. Simple things like giving up a seat for an elderly person shows how well-mannered, considerate and cultured you are. Honour God first, and then honour the rest of humanity by being courteous and respectful.

Ephesians 6:2-3
Amplified Bible (AMP)

Honour (esteem and value as precious) your father and your mother—this is the first commandment with a promise— That all may be well with you and that you may live long on the earth.

Respect your parents; treat them with honour, obedience, and courtesy. The Bible attaches a promise to this command, and the promise is long life! It's never becoming to talk back to your parents or shout at them. They are not your equals and will never be. Even when you feel they are in the wrong, ask God for wisdom on how to handle such a situation. When you feel that they are wrongly accusing you of a matter, keep your cool, be silent, and maintain respect and politeness. Trust me, God will reward you.

Respect those in authority and above you. Treat them with respect, and always remember that one day it will be your turn. What you do for others now is like a seed you are planting for your future. Be wise in your dealings.

1 Peter 5:5
New King James Version (NKJV)

Likewise you younger people, submit yourselves to your elders. Yes, all of you be submissive to one another, and be clothed with humility, for "God resists the proud, but gives grace to the humble."

Mind your manners: Learn to say *"Excuse me"*, *"I beg your pardon"*, *"May I"*, *"Please"*, and *"Thank you"*. Sometimes the people I come across forget these basic principles. Don't be rude in your interaction with others. Show gratitude and appreciation and make the other person feel bigger and respected. They will love you for it.

Here is an example: When you go to someone looking for lift into town and say, "Can I go with you into town?" you imply that the person has got no option but to just take you anyway. It's less polite. But when you say, "May I please go with you into town?" it's more polite. You are asking in a more respectful way, thereby letting the person know that you are aware of their right to say yes or no. It's more graceful to say "may I", and it puts you in favour with the next person.

Genuinely say "Thank you" to show appreciation and gratitude. You will get more favours in the future. A simple "please" can go a long way. Don't be rude.

Refrain from the use of bad language. Again, it's unbecoming! Know when to speak and when to shut your mouth. There is a time and place for everything.

Table manners: Manners include other things, like not using your mobile phone or reading whilst at the dinner table, or leaning on the table during meal times (especially if it's a formal occasion). It is simply not proper and elegant. No talking with your mouth full. Take time to chew your food. No one is chasing you. No slouching, but sit up straight, and eating whilst standing is a big no. Such things will prove beneficial when God expands your social and business circles, and you are invited to prestigious ceremonies. Always be on your guard and prepared. Start learning these things now. Know how to properly hold your fork and knife, and be well acquainted with how to use your cutlery in a formal setting. (Know which way to work the cutlery. Start from the outside going in; start with the utensils furthest away from your plate and work your way in *towards* your plate with each course.)

Salutations: Know how to properly address respectable people with their formal titles and position of authority. Always know the culture of the environment you are in to avoid offense. In some cultures you have to lower your eyes when speaking to elderly people or people in higher authority.

Pass that compliment: How do you make others feel? In conversation, be someone who makes others feel better about themselves. Make them feel important and highly esteemed. Be the person to leave someone feeling encouraged. As I said before, learn to pay a compliment. Everybody craves to be praised and appreciated. Let your approbation be heartfelt, and be generous with your compliments. You will be loved for your lavish praise towards others. If you have nothing good to say, then don't say anything at all.

> *You never know when a moment and a few*
> *sincere words can impact a life forever.*
> —Zig Ziglar

Dressing: Know the occasion, and dress appropriately for it. Don't turn up for an interview in your summer shorts (unless if the job calls for it) or for a church service in your evening wear. Play your cards right, and avoid the embarrassment and ridicule. Be polite in your dressing. Ladies need to dress modestly, like ladies, and avoid showing too much flesh; it is just not classy. As for guys, dropping your pants only reflects your character and manners. Nobody will respect such a person. Real gentlemen know how to dress appropriately. The way you dress will determine the level of respect you receive. Your dressing in general reflects on your manners as a person. Dressing well is a form of good manners. Get it right, and dress respectably.

Mobile phone etiquette: Be polite when talking to someone on the phone. Give your name when you answer the phone and smile too. Somehow a smile can transcend through a telephone conversation. Your smile carries sound and tone, and the next person can definitely feel the smile in the tone of your voice. Don't talk loudly in public. Never answer your phone during an important or formal meeting. Always set your phone to silent while out, such as the movies, restaurant, opera house, or play. Put your phone away and pay attention to those talking to you. It's called respect. When you text, please make use of proper grammar and punctuation. Shorthand typing can cripple your grammar and spelling ability. Be careful what you text. Some things are better said in person than sent as a text. Avoid lashing out on someone through a text message, because once sent, you can't take it back. In general, avoid responding to someone whilst angry as well. Cool down first and then speak with a sober mind.

Bathroom etiquette: Always remember to wash, brush, floss, and flush. It's all to do with the next person. Leave the bathing room in a condition you would like to find it yourself. Guys, when you miss your aim, please wipe off urine residue. Think of the next person. Nobody wants to come in and do it for you. It's disgusting.

> *Cleanliness and order are matters of education, and like most great things, you must cultivate a taste for them.*
> —Benjamin Disraeli

Online etiquette: Apply the netiquette rules.

N – Necessary: Do people really want to know what you are posting?

E – Exemplary: Are you portraying yourself in a model fashion?

T – Thought-provoking: Is your post stimulating?

I – Idealistic: Do your thoughts show principle?

Q – Quotable: If someone used the words in your post to define you, how would you be remembered?

U – Understandable: Can people understand what you are saying? What about your tone?

E – Essential: Is what you are saying critical to the conversation?

T – Trustworthy: Do you words portray you as someone in whom people can confide?

T – True: Is there truth in what you are saying? Never lie, it's unbecoming.

E – Exactly what you intend: Overall, does your post convey exactly what you intend to convey?

Never post something, write an email or letter while you are angry. Cool down first and then write sensibly.

In case you mingle with royalty: When meeting the King or Queen of England in particular, they must be addressed as "Your Majesty", followed by "Sir" or "Ma'am". The rest of the royal family are addressed as "Your Royal Highness", followed by "Sir" or "Ma'am". Unless the members of royalty extend their hand to you in greeting, never extend your hand to them, and don't take it personally if no hand is proffered.

Any dialogue with royalty requires that you gracefully allow them to steer the topics and direction of conversation. Asking direct questions is discouraged. Never ask anything too personal. When referring to a member of the royal family in conversation, use their title or honorific. Before you enter into royal circles, make sure your royal history and protocol is up to scratch. Royal protocol differs with each monarch. Know the rules of the circle you are invited to.

Common courtesy: This includes simple things as opening the door for someone, or for guys, pulling out a chair for your mother or sister or any lady at the dinner table. Other courtesies include offering to carry someone else's bags or simply making yourself profitable to someone else's benefit. Courtesy is also encouraged on the road, how you treat other drivers. Learn simple things as giving way to other drivers and keeping a cool head whilst on the road. Avoid losing your temper. Road rage is not ladylike or gentlemanly. Don't have a rowdy character. It is undesirable, makes you look a fool, and pushes people away from you. Be calm and composed! Courtesy involves everything else I've mentioned above and more. Courtesy is the core of etiquette.

In a nutshell: Say "please". Smile and greet adults. Use your inside voice. Sit up straight. Dress to impress. "May I" is more polite than "Can I". Interact politely. Behave decently. Work Patiently. Chew with your mouth closed and take your time. Write thank-you notes and show gratitude. Wait your turn. Give good compliments, and take compliments courteously. Use kind words. Keep a napkin on your lap at dinner tables. Respect differences. Ask for permission. Say "excuse me". Clean up after yourself. Open doors for others. Know how to behave in the presence of royalty. And finally, say "thank you".

Some Etiquette Nuggets:

➢ *Politeness is a sign of dignity, not subservience.* —Theodore Roosevelt

➢ *Choose your words carefully. Once spoken they can only be forgiven, never forgotten.* —David Conellias

➢ *Etiquette is the science of living. It embraces everything. It is ethics. It is honour.* —Emily Post

➢ *It is nice to be important, but it's more important to be nice.* —John Cassis

➢ *Good manners will often take people where neither money nor education will take them.* —David Conellias

➢ *No matter who you are or what you do, your manners will have a direct impact on your professional and social success.* —David Conellias

➢ *Be curious, not judgemental.* —David Conellias

➢ *Manners make the man.* —David Conellias

➢ *Respect is earned, honesty is appreciated, trust is gained, and loyalty is returned. When someone is loyal to you, it is only fair and honourable to return the favour.* —David Conellias

➢ *Good manners open closed doors; bad manners close the open door.* —Mehmet Murat IIdan

➢ *Good manners are just a way of showing other people that we have respect for them.* —Bill Kelly

➢ *Politeness and consideration for others is like investing pennies and getting dollars back.* —Thomas Sowell

➢ *Every action done in company ought to be with some sign of respect to those that are present.* —George Washington

➢ *Don't reserve your best behaviour for special occasions. You can't have two sets of manners, two social codes – one for those you admire and want to impress, another for those whom you consider unimportant. You must be the same to all people.* —Lillian Eichler Watson

➢ *Manners cost nothing, lack of them costs everything!* —David Conellias

Principle #18:

COMMUNICATE WELL

Actions speak louder than words.

Communication (from the Latin *commūnicāre*, meaning "to share") is an integral part of human life. It is a way of conveying information through the exchange of ideas, feelings, intentions, attitudes, expectations, perceptions or commands, as by speech, gestures, writings, behaviour, and various other means. When people fail to communicate, relationships and bonds wither away and die. Communication is a way that people can stay connected and united. When we properly communicate, the bonds of love we share are made stronger and stronger by the day.

Communication can be conveyed through verbal or non-verbal forms, such as body language, eye contact, haptic communication, and sign language, as well as media content, such as pictures, graphics, sound, and writing. Simply put, a text message, even conventional letters, emails, phone calls, taking time out with friends, a handshake, hugging, holding hands, a hearty smile, a look in the eye, the list is endless, these are all different manners of communication. Communication skills differ at every level and stage in life.

When it comes to intimacy, some skills are only meant for married couples; some are meant to be shared between friends and family. Use your discretion, be careful not to send a skill out of your level, and don't send the wrong signals or vibes! A communication skill out of time and season can lead to the wrong and undesired outcome. Bottom line: avoid carnality, and know when and where to use your skills.

Communication requires that the communicating parties share an area of communicative commonality. The communication process is complete once the receiver understands the sender's message. When the receiver fails to understand the sender's intentions, that's when misunderstandings spring up.

When communicating, it's always important to convey your message clearly to avoid misunderstandings. And as the receiver, always aim to understand the sender's intentions before making a conclusion, especially if communication is unclear.

A Closer Look

Body language: They say actions speak louder than words. When it comes to body language, be careful that the words you convey correspond with your actions. Otherwise you might say something really nice to someone, but if your body language suggest the opposite, the person is more likely to believe your actions more than your words! Let not your words contradict your actions, but let both match up. Be careful with your handshakes; let them be firm and reassuring. Let your hugs be heartfelt and warm.

Have a good posture, especially when attending an interview. Sit up straight and don't slouch. Guys, don't spread your legs too far apart as if you are watching a football match at home Somehow it just looks unprofessional.

Your eyes are the windows to your soul; keep eye contact to show the next person you are serious and interested in whatever they might be saying. When it comes to eye contact, it differs from culture to culture. Some cultures consider it rude to look your elders in the eye. It's worth noting your environment and not to offend by passing the wrong gestures. And also be careful whom you make eye contact with and what the occasion for making eye contact is. Some people might take it the wrong way, especially when it comes to the opposite sex.

Verbal language: A child of God should never cuss, let alone anybody else. It's demeaning to your personage! Mind your language; let your speech be seasoned with salt and grace (Colossians 4:6). A fowl mouth and perverse lips are a reproach to the Lord. Mind what comes out of your mouth. It speaks volumes about your character and depletes your dignity. You lose the people's respect and honour!

Facial expressions: Your face says it all! Facial expressions can make someone feel welcome or turn a potential friend away. Your face is usually the first point of contact to give away how you are feeling at a particular moment. Your facial expressions can signal if you are feeling happy, sad, moody, annoyed, grumpy or just overjoyed to see someone. Your face gives it all away. When you are not being genuine in your smiling, most people can easily pick that up. Be wary of the expressions you make when around others. Of all the things you can wear, your expression is the most important!

Keeping up appearances: Have a good clothing/fashion sense. The way you dress also communicates what type of person you are! Dress like you want to be addressed. People can easily assume someone's position in life just by simply looking at the way they dress. The way you dress can make people assume whether you are a businessman/-woman, a hippy, a gangster, or royalty. Your dressing speaks volumes about you. I've noticed that every time I walk into the bank wearing a tie, they always address me respectfully as "Sir" or "Mr", but when I don't, they just address me casually with my first name "David". That taught me a great deal.

Technology and social media: Technology when used wisely is good. It is an efficient and quick way of communication and proves beneficial for long-distance relationships. But I believe it's not supposed to totally replace conventional methods of communication and bonding with each other. Technology should never surpass our human interaction. We now have a generation that is connected and yet so disconnected. Social media has taken over quality family time. Electronic impulses are highly regarded, rather than the effective physical presence of special and dear company. This generation is obsessed with *"gadgets"*, as my father says. People are now overly concerned with keeping a perfect image on social media, and getting more "Likes" on Facebook or Instagram, rather than spending more time in the *presence* of those dear to them, or let alone more time with God.

Trust me, physical contact and presence goes a longer way than electronic connection. Technology is giving birth to a generation of dull and lonely people. Just because you have over a thousand friends on Facebook does not mean that each one of them is truly there for you or interested in you. It does not secure or guarantee satisfaction in life; it just feeds your vanity. Be watchful of how much time you spend on these gadgets. They are not meant to control you; you are supposed to control them. Technology has become the modern-day slavery. Imagine being handcuffed to your phone or tablet by choice, or being late for meetings, work, or informal appointments with loved ones just because you were busy on Facebook or Instagram. What a waste of precious time doing something unproductive. I am not saying technology is bad, but learn the art of moderation. Everything should have its place and time. Keep a balanced scale! The gadget should never be your god or master. You are supposed to be in charge of it. Build stronger relationships and bonds by learning to *switch off* and giving more attention to what really matters in life. When around friends and family, put away the gadgets and focus on them instead. Their company is more precious than social media.

> *It has become appallingly obvious that our technology has exceeded our humanity.*
> —Albert Einstein

Purpose in your heart to have god communication skills!

Principle #19:

PRAISE AND WORSHIP

Remember the tea kettle – it is always up to its
neck in hot water, yet it still sings.
—Crystal Rosales

This is one of my favourite topics, because I love to sing, I am passionate about music, in particular worship music. The Bible is clear when it says God "inhabits" the praises of His people. God loves it when we praise and worship Him. Imagine Him being drawn to the sweet sound of music and praise coming from our hearts, and taking a seat in the midst of the sweet smelling aroma of your praise, just to watch you pour out your love on Him. How will that make Him feel? Imagine Him being your lover, coming to give you a kiss in response to your kind words of praise. I know for a fact that when God kisses you, things will never be the same in your life, and I can testify to that. If we as humans love to be praised and appreciated, how about God Himself?

When we wholeheartedly praise and worship the King, we demonstrate before His presence our gratitude and appreciation to the King for His favour, security, and privileges of being in His kingdom. When we worship Him, we demonstrate how valuable the King is to us. To praise and worship is to show warm approval or admiration of. It is to commend, applaud, pay tribute, speak highly, eulogise, compliment, celebrate, sing the praises, rave, take one's hat off, hail, glorify, honour, exalt, adore, hallow, bless, venerate, revere, show devotion, esteem highly, honour, show respect, render homage, extol, laud, adulate, idolise, cherish, treasure, hold in high regard, hold in awe and look up to. The list is endless. All these definitions show the attitude that we ought to have before His presence.

A Clean Heart

Just like prayer, it is imperative that we allow the Holy Spirit to cleanse our hearts and flush out all the toxins that might hinder freedom in worship. Approach the throne of grace with a clean sincere heart. "Create in me a clean heart, o God, and renew the right spirit within me," David cries in Psalm 51. David understood the importance of a clean heart and the right attitude before the presence of God. A heart cluttered with toxins (grudges, anger, resentment, unforgiveness, and bitterness) and unwillingness to yield to the cleansing of the Spirit breed the wrong attitude before His presence. Lift up your left hand in surrender to God and touch your heart with your right hand asking the Holy Spirit to dispose of any dirt and clutter that might hinder a breakthrough. It is your duty to set things right! Sweep over my soul Holy Spirit, and let your living waters flow over my soul as you take control. Take heed and worship with the right set of mind for God to manifest Himself to you and in you.

The Relationship Factor

God is after a relationship with us and not after religion. I love it when the Bible says that God rejoices over us with singing. When I think of that Scripture, I always wonder what kind of song God sings over me. What causes Him to rejoice over me with gladness and quiet me with His love when my soul is troubled? For someone to rejoice over you with singing and gladness of heart, there has to be more than just a mere relationship. There has to be an intimate connection. A deep intimate connection causes someone to have gladness in their heart when they think of you. Now that is real love! And what I know is that a good relationship is fruitful and mutually beneficial. It's a two-way thing. Both parties should be at the receiving and giving ends; both parties should benefit. If only one party is benefitting and not both, then the relationship is not balanced, and therefore the bond can easily be weakened leading to a breakup. When you truly love someone, then giving the person your all is never a problem. You are willing to do whatever it takes to please that person, even if it means risking your very own life.

When I sing to Him (appreciate and acknowledge Him) and give Him my praise, worship, adoration, time, heart, substance, as well as the very essence and being of myself, He gladly sings back to me and rejoices over me by adorning me with His goodness, favour, mercy, and grace. We have just the perfect example of God's love song to us through Song of Solomon. Song of Solomon illustrates the intimate relationship God desires to have with us the bride/church as our husband and maker (Isaiah 54:5).

Zephaniah 3:17
New King James Version (NKJV)

The LORD your God in your midst,
The Mighty One, will save;
He will rejoice over you with gladness,
He will quiet you with His love,
He will rejoice over you with singing.

Imagine singing heartily for some friends and showering them with praise, but they in turn say nothing at all to show gratitude or appreciation. How would that make you feel? I guess embarrassed and humiliated, right? Now God is the lover who will never want to humiliate you when you rejoice over Him with singing, He responds by singing joyfully over you as well. When it comes to etiquette, God is the Master. He is polite, merciful, gentle, kind, all-loving, and all-knowing. Above all, He responds to our call of intimacy. Praising and worshipping God requires that we do it with a certain level of intimacy that springs forth from the depths of our hearts. We ought to revere Him in all His awesomeness and majestic power. When you acknowledge His infinite power through song, He dances to your beautiful music, and when he dances within your territory, I can assure you that your enemies (anything that has come against you) will be put to flight! Trust me on this. When you sing to Him, He sings back to you, and when He dances to your beautiful music, no enemy can stand in front of you! Now that's refreshing isn't it?

Sometimes we face hurdles and struggles in life to the point where our praise gets chocked up, and we lose sight of our Husband and Maker. Let me tell you something. Don't stop singing His praise because of circumstances. Rather than focusing on the storm, focus on giving God even more praise, because by doing so, you invite Him in the midst of your storm, and eventually He will calm it down and still the raging winds. The trick here is having patience in the midst of it all and never backing down from your faith and trust in Him. Singing to Him, or worshipping Him, will calm your fears. It glorifies and exonerates God rather than magnifying the situation, because sometimes we forget how powerful and magnificent God is and magnify the situations that torment us more than God. God is never God *small mighty* but God *Almighty*. Praise and worship are expressions of our faith. When we praise and worship Him, we put flesh on our faith and improve its impact! Never allow situations around you belittle the magnificence of the Almighty God. Keep singing and praising even when you feel the flames getting hotter. It's only a matter of time before God pours water all over them. Patience and consistent faith are key here. Shout in praise at the walls that have stood against your will and purpose; command them to come down through your praise!

Expressing honour and adoration towards God can be done in many ways. It can be the lifting up of hands or a simple clap. It can be dancing or playing an instrument. To Him it's all beautiful. Let's take a look at some Hebrew praise terms that could help us during our worship moments.

Hebrew Praise Terms

Halal: The word *Hallelujah* comes from this term. It means to be clear, to shine, to boast, to rave, to show, and to celebrate. It is the root word for praise in Hebrew. (Psalm 113:1–3; 149:3; 150:1)

Psalm 113:1
Amplified Bible (AMP)

*Praise the Lord! (Hallelujah!) Praise, O servants of the Lord, praise [**Halal**] the name of the Lord!*

Yadah: It is verb with a root meaning *to throw out the hand, the extended hand*. It therefore means *to worship with extended hands*. Extended hands can be a sign of giving thanks to the Lord. (2 Chronicles 20:21; Psalm 22:22; 63:1; 69:30; 107:15)

2 Chronicles 20:21
Amplified Bible (AMP)

*When he had consulted with the people, he appointed singers to sing to the Lord and praise Him in their holy [priestly] garments as they went out before the army, saying, give thanks to the Lord [**yadah**], for His mercy and loving-kindness endure forever!*

Towdah: Comes from the same principle root word as *yadah* but is used more specifically. The words literally mean *an extension of the hand in humble adoration, acceptance, or avowal*. It is used for thanking God for things not yet received, and for those already at hand. (Psalm 42:4; 50:14; 50:23; Jeremiah 33:11)

Psalm 50:23

Amplified Bible (AMP)

*He who brings an offering of praise [towdah] and thanksgiving
honours and glorifies Me; and he who orders his way
aright [who prepares the way that I may show him], to
him I will demonstrate the salvation of God.*

Shabach: *Shabach* means *to shout, to address in a loud tone, or to triumph.*
(Psalm 35:27; 47:1; 63:1–4; 145:4; Isaiah 12:6)

Psalm 47:1

Amplified Bible (AMP)

*O clap your hands, all you peoples! Shout [**Shabach**] to
God with the voice of triumph and songs of joy!*

Barak: *Barak is kneeling down, blessing God as an act of adoration.* (1
Chronicles 29:20; Job 1:21; Psalm 34:1; 95:6). Where is says
"bless", use the term *barak*.

Psalm 34:1

Amplified Bible (AMP)

*I will bless [**barak**] the Lord at all times; His
praise shall continually be in my mouth.*

Zamar: To *zamar* is to *pluck the strings of an instrument, to sing, to
praise.* It's a musical word which is largely involved with joyful
expressions of music with musical instruments. (1 Chronicles
16:9; Psalm 27:6; 57:8–9; Isaiah 12:5)

Psalm 21:13

Amplified Bible (AMP)

*Be exalted, Lord, in Your strength; we will sing
and praise [**zamar**] Your power.*

Tehillah: *Tehillah* is derived from the word *halal;* it means *the singing
of halals, to sing or to laud.* It is perceived to involve music,
especially singing hymns of the Spirit (prophetic worship).
(Isaiah 61:3; Psalm 33:1;, Isaiah 61:3, Psalm 147:1–2)

Psalm 22:3

(Amplified Bible (AMP)

*But You are holy, O You Who dwell in [the holy place
where] the praises [**tehillah**] of Israel [are offered].*

THE POWER OF PRAISE
AND WORSHIP

Praise Confuses the Enemy:

2 Chronicles 20:22–23
New King James Version (NKJV)

Now when they began to sing and to praise, the LORD set ambushes against the people of Ammon, Moab, and Mount Seir, who had come against Judah; and they were defeated. For the people of Ammon and Moab stood up against the inhabitants of Mount Seir to utterly kill and destroy them. And when they had made an end of the inhabitants of Seir, they helped to destroy one another.

Read the rest of 2 Chronicles 20:1–27. From the accounts of 2 Chronicles 20, when the children of Israel faced with a great multitude of warriors so fierce, instead of going into panic mode, the Levites from the children of the Kohatithes of the children of the Korahites stood up to praise the Lord God of Israel with voices *loud* and *high* (*shabach*). Then Jehoshaphat appointed those who should sing to the Lord (*zamar/tehillah*) and who should praise the beauty of holiness. They praised the "mercy" of the Lord, saying it endures forever. God responded by setting ambushes against their enemies, as He had promised them victory beforehand. Their enemies ended up fighting each other and destroying themselves. All this happened whilst Israel simply sang and praised God. They did not even have to get blood on their hands!

Look at how Jehoshaphat addressed the Lord (2 Chronicles 20:5–13) with the issue which was before them, how he exalted God Almighty and pleaded with Him, and how God responded through the prophet Jahaziel, promising them victory. Judah received a word from the Lord, promising them victory beforehand. That was reason enough for them to go crazy and start praising God, because the victory was already won. God had promised that they "need not" fight in this battle, for the battle belonged to God.

Now that's a lesson for us, too. Whatever enemy might have risen up against you and caused you fear or dismay, rise up, ascribe greatness and majesty to the Lord, and believe that you have the victory already. The Word says, "We are more than conquerors through Christ Jesus" (2 Chronicles 20:5–13). Start praising the beauty of Holiness, sing of God's mercy, and praise Him. He will surely come to your rescue without you having to sweat it. The word of encouragement is given already through His Word. Use that Word to your advantage. Believe in the power of God, and let Him put things in order for you. All you have to do is *shabach, zamar, tehillah, yadah*, and believe!

When faced with Goliath, David did not succumb to the threats or the sounds his enemy (Goliath) was making. Whilst others saw terror dawning on them and shrieked in the sight of Goliath with fear, David heard the sound of victory roaring in the streets instead. He affirmed His bold stance and faith in God through the words He spoke in exoneration towards God (1 Samuel 17:45–51). A worshipper knows and trusts in the power of the Almighty God no matter how big or small the situation. When Saul tried to discourage David in verse 33, saying that he was a youth, David did not stand down from his unwavering faith in God. David was firmly anchored in the goodness and supernatural might of God. He did not lower his theology to match the fear of Saul's army. How anchored are you in God's goodness, might, and supernatural abilities? God would not allow Saul's armour to fit on David, because He wanted to prove His supernatural power and abilities as Jehovah Gibbor and Jehovah Sabbaoth in support of David's faith towards Him. The hand of God had to be clear in all of this. A true worshipper is known by the words they utter in affirmation of God's power. When others see fear, the worshipper sees an opportunity for God's power to be demonstrated.

Praise vs. the Distressing Spirit

1 Samuel 16:23

New King James Version (NKJV)

And so it was, whenever the distressing spirit from God was upon Saul, that David would take a harp and play it with his hand. Then Saul would become refreshed and well, and the distressing spirit would depart from him.

In accounts of the story of David and Saul, we find that whenever Saul got attacked by the distressing spirit, He would call out for David to come and play his harp (*zamar*). The reason Saul received the distressing spirit from God was because of disobedience. (Read the rest of 1 Samuel 16 to see the bigger picture.) As we know, David worshipped God in song and on his harp (*zamar*) ever since he was young, tending his father's sheep. Whenever he would play his harp for Saul, the distressing spirit would depart from Saul, and Saul would become refreshed and well again. Even though Saul would try and kill David with his javelin in the process, David would always get the strength to dodge the spear of his enemy, and the spear of his enemy never prevailed against him. David would behave wisely in the presence of his enemy. Through him we have most of the psalms we recite and read today. Whenever David was in trouble, he knew his power lied within his praise and adoration towards God. No wonder God calls him "the man after His own heart". David would always seek after God through all of his struggles.

When the enemy throws his spear at you, let his fiery darts be quenched by your faith in praise towards God. Dodge the enemy's javelin by praying and declaring God's Word against his tactics, but don't stop singing your song. Continue to *zamar* until your enemies are confounded and subdued. Even when all sorts of aggravating situations come against you, let your soul continue to bless the Lord till all is well. Even when all is well, your praise should remain continuous and constant. When Saul throws his javelin at you, don't come down to his level and give away your power, but arise and fight back with praise towards the Most High. This might make the enemy even more angry and confused, but don't quit. Because when God (*El-Gibbor, El-Sabbaoth*) intervenes, it's all sweet victory. All the things that might have tried to bring distress to you, flee at the presence of the Almighty. When Light (God) finally arrives to your rescue, every bit of darkness instantly disappears.

Above all, even when you own soul is distressed, give a *zamar* praise to God and feel His power enlighten you. A *zamar* praise can lift off heavy burdens; it calms your spirit. There's always something soothing about worship music, especially when played on any stringed instrument. It has the power to heal and refresh your spirit. Every time you go into your closet, have some time to either play an instrument in worship or listen to soothing worship music as you focus your heart on God.

Power of Agreement in Prayer and Praise

Acts 16:25–26

New King James Version (NKJV)

But at midnight Paul and Silas were praying and singing hymns to God, and the prisoners were listening to them. Suddenly there was a great earthquake, so that the foundations of the prison were shaken; and immediately all the doors were opened and everyone's chains were loosed.

When Paul and Silas were put in prison, in a pit so deep and dark that there was no chance of escape, all they had were their voices and each other. They had the power of making melody in their hearts unto the King of Kings (Ephesians 5:9). The Bible says, "When two or more of you agree, touching anything in heaven and on earth, it shall be done" (Matthew 18:19). Whenever there's agreement, one accord, and unity, God has no option but to *command* a blessing. The blessing comes in different forms. In the case of Paul and Silas, they were tightly bound by *heavy* chains, which no ordinary hand could break. The security around them was very tight and of the highest level, according to the measures of those roman times. And the Bible says, when midnight came, Paul and Silas prayed and sang hymns to God. Even the prisoners heard them. Suddenly, there was a great earthquake, so that the foundations of the prison were shaken. Immediately all the doors were opened, and everyone else's chains were loosed. Because Paul and Silas were honourable men of God, they did not escape but maintained integrity. Reading this Scripture in Acts 16 made me leap for joy. God is great! I always imagine that the earthquake was caused by God tapping His feet to Paul and Silas's songs. They got God excited and pleased with their *united* and *sincere* sacrifice of praise. God had no option but to act, especially after seeing such singleness of heart and agreement Paul and Silas had.

What is it that has bound you up? What situation is it that seems too impossible to conquer? Even when the enemy *tries* to put us in chains, remember that we have weapons of mass destruction called *prayer* and *praise*. The reason people who endured the slave trade made it through those difficult times was they understood the power of making melody. When life was tough and unbearable, music made their burden somehow bearable and kept them going. They would sing their way through pain until the day of emancipation finally arrived. This is the power in music. When the enemy has put you in a prison cell, where you feel so trapped and confined that you *think* there's no way out, praise your way out! Your praise is the "shackle breaker". You must always carry it with you wherever you go, always making melody and singing spiritual songs with thanksgiving in your heart. Paul and Silas prayed and praised their way out of the heavy chains that bound them. Even the people around them were affected by their praise. Have you ever praised God so much that when He answers, the answer affects your surroundings and everybody else connected to you? You might be the answer that someone else is looking for. Don't stop the praise. Praise until something happens; make melody in your heart unto the King of Kings without ceasing. Be the one to loose someone else's bonds through your melody of praise. Find a partner to agree with when it comes to some of these stubborn matters, because when there is agreement, things definitely happen. I know this for myself; trust me! Be the one to cause an earthquake because of your prayers and praise. Boldly *declare* victory, and watch your confidence in God rewarded.

2 Chronicles 5:13–14

New King James Version (NKJV)

Indeed it came to pass, when the trumpeters and singers were as one, to make one sound to be heard in praising and thanking the LORD, and when they lifted up their voice with the trumpets and cymbals and instruments of music, and praised the LORD, saying:

"For He is good, or His mercy endures forever,"

That the house, the house of the LORD, was filled with a cloud, so that the priests could not continue ministering because of the cloud; for the glory of the LORD filled the house of God.

If we want to experience the glory of the Lord in reality during our praise and worship, oneness is of paramount importance. I cannot emphasise enough how God values unity. When people are not united, our worship towards Him can never be fulfilled. True fulfilment comes when we experience His glory to the extent that we see the results manifesting in the physical realm, affecting our surroundings. Even when alone, your focus is important as well. you can't expect a manifestation when your body, soul, and spirit are not in agreement with what you are trying to achieve (e.g., trying to worship God whilst paying attention to your mobile phone; already there's a disconnection). Your whole body and being need to be one with your spirit in order to see the results of your intimate time with God.

Worship and the Prophetic:

2 Kings 3:15
New King James Version (NKJV)

But now bring me a musician.
Then it happened, when the musician played, that
the hand of the Lord came upon him.

Clearly it's quite evident that when you *zamar* or *tehillah*, or praise and worship God in any form, you invoke His presence, and His glory shines upon you. Once you get into that beautiful space, you begin to get ushered into the prophetic. The Lord starts to speak to you and reveal what's on His heart. Once you reach into the realm of the prophetic, everything is laid bare. You begin to see things that other people don't see; you begin to hear things that other people don't hear. It's like the climax of your intimate time with the Lord. When you live such a lifestyle of praise and worship, you are untouchable, even other people will notice the difference, and they will be able to smell God all around you. Desire to reach such a stage in your worship time with the Lord. Allow the Spirit to usher you, and obey that voice steering you in the direction you ought to take during your worship time. Prophets love this realm, because it's home for them. Even Elisha called for a musician, so that the musician could *zamar*, and Elisha would prophesy. Let your music lead you into that zone behind the veil where there are no negotiations for miracles.

The Ark of His Presence

As I've mentioned before, many times when the Children of Israel were faced with an enemy, singers and musicians would be appointed to go ahead of the congregation carrying the ark of God's presence. As they would praise the beauty of holiness, the Lord would fight their battles in a supernatural way not comprehended by man. As the Lord's temples, we are supposed to house the ark of His presence in ourselves, just like the ark back then was housed in the temple's Holy of Holies. God's presence is supposed to dwell richly in us, and praising and worshipping God is a very effective way of invoking God's presence, because He indwells the praises of His people. Decide to always carry this ark for victory! No one dares mess with the one who carries God's presence. (Romans 8:31: "If God is for us, who can be against us?", for "greater is He that is in us, than He that is in the world." 1 John 4:4). Check to be sure that He is inside of you, and then you can boast of His might.

The one who carries His presence attracts the blessing. You find that in the Bible, blessing would follow the nation, city, or house where God's ark resided. Look at the house of Obed Edom: he became blessed when he humbly and gladly received the ark into his home. King David heard of this and earnestly sought the safe return of the ark to Zion (Jerusalem). David desired for the emblem of God's presence to dwell within the city walls of Jerusalem. He understood that the nation's protection and prosperity depended upon the return of the ark of God's presence. When the ark was returned, David danced to the point where he did not care about being dignified. This displeased his wife Michal, but in turn God was displeased by Michal's reaction, and her womb was shut from bearing children! Who are you to be displeased by someone else's praise offering to God? Be careful you don't judge how someone worships God, because you might block your own blessing and peace! Having the wrong attitude always costs! But God in His mercy and kindness is always longsuffering and loving towards us and gives us countless chances to get it right.

When you carry "The Presence," people will notice something different and unique about you; they will be able to literally sense that positive supernatural aura around you. When you carry "The Presence", you carry the energy that causes healing to take place, and you positively impact the people around you. People you come across will be able to sense and experience the presence of the divine shalom (peace), because the one who gives the peace that surpasses all understanding will be residing in you. When you praise and worship Him, you invoke His divine presence and all that is attached to Him. And you will not negotiate for your needs to be met, because the one who provides it all will be dwelling in you and will be upon you. He brings all that He has to offer to the one who is willing to yield to Him in worship and adoration. You'll find that when you are in His presence, you thrive and truly function to your maximum potential, which was God's original intention and plan when He created the Garden of Eden (the garden of His presence; Ezekiel 28:13), for man to dwell in. This was where God's presence touched the earth! Just as every creature needs oxygen to survive, going without God is like going without oxygen; you are as good as dead. When you don't have the presence, you don't have peace, and you easily succumb to life's worries and cares, because the Giver of life itself isn't in you.

Purpose in your heart to lead a worship-driven lifestyle!

Principle #20:

KEEP JESUS AT THE CENTRE

Christ is like the nucleus that holds the atom together. And we are like the electrons that orbit this nucleus in atomic shells.
—Munashe Chibwe

The word *attraction* comes from the Latin word *attrahere*, which in our modern English language means the action or power of evoking interest in, or liking for, someone or something. In scientific terms, it is used to describe a force under the influence of which objects tend to move towards each other. Gravitational attraction is an example of this.

Think of when you were a baby, and your parents or older siblings and other family members used to throw you in the air and catch you as you fell towards those caring arms. Without gravitational attraction, you would have drifted off, maybe even into space. Hence the attraction, or pull of gravity, is important to us beings on earth.

As much as gravity is important to us, the attraction between us and our Father in heaven is a whole lot more important, and is in fact quite pivotal on our journey to *real* life. That is why when we had "drifted" away from Him through Adam, He gave us a second chance through His only begotten Son, Jesus Christ, the "Second Adam". Jesus Christ came and paid the ultimate price on the cross at Calvary, so that the gap between us and our Heavenly Father might be bridged. (Romans 3:23)

In doing so, that force of attraction was restored, and we can now approach His throne boldly, because when the Father looks at us, all He sees is the blood of Jesus Christ covering us, and Christ's righteousness shining through us. Now this is the grace of God that we have received through Christ Jesus our Lord and Saviour. His grace is indeed sufficient for us (2 Corinthians 12:9)

You'll find that in life, sometimes we start to move away from this unmerited favour by some of the things we do or say. This is that human nature (flesh) which is constantly at war with the spirit; hence the well-known saying "no one is perfect". But this should never be an excuse for us for sin and error. In the midst of the constant battle, thank God He gave us the Holy Spirit as a guide and leader who makes us aware of this "drift". Once conviction kicks in, we go back to our prayer closets and seek redemption and forgiveness. It is when we ignore the warning signs of this drift away from our Father that things begin to go berserk (insane, out of control, crazy, unbearable).

A Little Bit of Chemistry

Fig 1.3: © Snapgalleria | Dreamstime.com - Atom Structure Photo

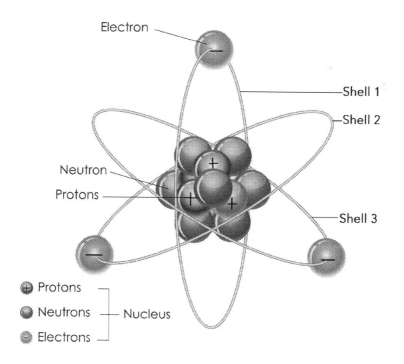

I'm reminded of the laws of attraction between protons and electrons in an atom of an element. The proton is a positively charged particle found in the nucleus (core) of the atom together with neutrons, and they are collectively known as nucleons. Whilst the electron is a negatively charged particle found in the atom's electron shells that orbit the nucleus. There is a force of attraction between these two particles called *nuclear attraction*. This force of attraction is caused by the opposite *but* "complementary" charges of the two particles. This force of attraction is responsible for the different trends in ionisation energies of different elements on the periodic table.

When we go down a particular group on the periodic table, we notice that the ionisation energies decrease. For example, the first ionisation energy of the element lithium is 520.2kj/mol-1, whilst the first ionisation energy of the element caesium is 370.7kj/mol-1. This is because the number of electron shells, as well as distance between the protons in the nucleus and outer electrons, increase. This will lead to the two particles experiencing a lower force of attraction, just like when you increase the distance between two magnets. This is caused by the *shielding effect* of electrons. As a result of this weaker force of attraction, a little amount of energy is required to remove the outer electrons from the atom's valence shell, or the outermost shell of the atom. The further away you are from the nucleus, the more likely you are to be "*expelled*" or "*disconnected*" from the atom in its entirety. The electrons in the outer shell don't feel the pull of the nucleus as strongly as those that are close to the nucleus. How close are you to this nucleus then? (Some of you have already got the revelation behind.)

This is the same in our everyday lives. We go through situations that may draw us away from God, and therefore we drift from His presence. When this drift happens, we are drawn away from the "positive nucleus" (which is God), and as a result we experience this shielding effect. When drawn away, just like the decrease in energy levels, we become weakened and are susceptible to attacks of any sorts. (I'm reminded of the teaching about how God is like a fireplace. The closer you are to Him, the warmer you get, and the more little flies and bugs stay away from you because of their resistance to the heat. The fire protects you from life's irritants.) When we become conformed to the desires of the flesh, it's easy for the electron to be removed from the atom's valence shell. (We lose God's covering, because darkness and light cannot coexist. One has to give way.)

On the other hand, as we go across the periodic table, we notice that the ionisation energies increase. In other words, there's an increase in atomic charge (think of it as a nuclear take over). For example, the first ionisation energy of lithium is 520.2kj/mol-1, whilst the first ionisation energy of fluorine is 1681.0kj/mol-1. This is because, as we go across a period, the number of electron shells *decreases* and the number of protons *increases*. The nuclear attraction will therefore increase between the protons and electrons, by increasing ionisation energy. This greater nuclear attraction pulls the electrons in more closely, thus forming some form of big *"nuclear hug"* because the electrons are pulled in closer to the nucleus. Remember the protons are found in the nucleus which represents Christ, and we are like the electrons that are drawn to Him through His love toward us, as long as we are willing to yield and surrender to His Spirit. Because of the intense level of attraction going on now, a whole lot of energy and effort will be required to overcome the attraction and separate the electron from the atom.

This concept is the same in our lives. When we continue to wait (as in serve) on the Lord, working in His house and being profitable to His kingdom. When we continue in the labour of love and follow His ways, He will hide us under the shadow of His wings and protect us. Just like the nucleus that holds the atom together, as long as we keep Him at the centre, He will hold everything that concerns our life in place. As long as we stay intensely attracted to Him, no matter what comes our way, no matter what the enemy tries to throw at us, nothing will be able to separate us from the love of the Father. Christ is the force majeure, and everything that might try to torment us has to bow to this greater force. Therefore brothers and sisters, be encouraged and let us strive to make God the centre (nucleus of protons) in our lives. Remain prayerful to keep the connection and attraction active, and like my father says, always remember that "God answers knee mail".

Read Deuteronomy 33:29; Psalm 17:8; 23; 27:1–5; 32:7; 37: 39–40; 91; 37:39–40; Luke 10:27; Romans 8:31–39

Jesus in Basketball

Being a huge fan of basketball, growing up, I would watch players like Michael Jordan, Scottie Pippen, Tim Duncan, Ray Allen, Kobe Bryant, Lebron James, and Kevin Durant. All I was interested in were the clutch 3s to beat the buzzer at the end of the game (Ray Allen's 3 in game 6 of the 2013 finals against San Antonio), and the dunks especially, but it never occurred to me how we can relate this wonderful game of basketball to our lives with Jesus Christ.

In an official basketball game (FIBA or NBA), the rules state that there can only be five players on the court, the point guard referred to as 1, the shooting guard referred to as the 2, the small forward referred to as the 3, the power forward or the 4, and the centre also known as the 5.

Our main focus in the game is the centre or the 5, otherwise abbreviated as the C, and coming back to biblical algebra, the number 5 represents the grace of God. Isn't it ironic that even the word *grace* itself contains 5 letters and so does the word MERCY, and in this scenario the letter C represents Christ, who is Jesus the centre of our salvation. If you look closely at it, *C* is also the third letter of the alphabet, and we now know that 3 represents the trinity (divine completion).

In the sport of basketball, there are many players who have thrived in their roles as the centres of their teams, for example Shaquille O'Neal, Tim Duncan, Chris Bosh, and Dwight Howard. This was because of their ability to "block" shots attempted by the opposing teams, guarding the post (painted area near the basket), taking jump balls to win possession, and their high rebounding numbers per game. It could be the difference between losing and winning a game, and so this proves why centres are pivotal in the team and therefore are the anchors of the team.

In our lives, Jesus Christ has to play the role of the centre by blocking shots from the enemy and protecting us from the opposing team (the enemy and his forces) trying to score points (Psalms 91, Romans 8:31). His aim is to rebound the ball, in an effort to win possession, and give us a second chance (plays) when we fall short. (Luke 15:11–32). It is important to know which team you are playing for and to be loyal to that team, because both teams have got their centres, and their aims are to win souls to their side. The choice is yours to choose which team you would rather belong to. Christ however is the greater force and everything bows to His name!

The centre is also referred to as the *big man* because of their sheer size and strength of these players. The centre uses his strength and size to defend anywhere on the court especially the post. This is the same with Jesus Christ as the anchor of our lives, our defender. He was given all power in heaven and on earth, and he has the name that is above every other name, on which when we call; we receive protection, healing, total deliverance, and divine provision. Therefore brothers and sisters, let us be encouraged in the power that Jesus Christ our Lord possesses. Like the Bible says, He can do exceedingly, abundantly above all that we can ever ask or think of or imagine, and most importantly, His agape love is the banner that watches over us. He is indeed the anchor, the pivot, and centre of our lives.

Rivers of Living Water: Come and Drink

When you have Jesus Christ in you, rivers of living waters flow out of you (by the Holy Spirit) and you will never thirst (lack) again. Your thirst (lack in every aspect of life) is quenched (you shall not want). You become a wellspring of life; everything around becomes affected by the waters of life flowing out through you. You will notice growth and greenness all around because your garden has got the waters of life watering it. Where the land was barren and penurious, there will be fruitfulness and vibrancy of life. When you have Him, you have every reason to live and enjoy life, because He makes all things beautiful. Even as you go through the valley of the shadow of death, you will see beauty amidst the chaos.

And guess what? The gift of salvation is free to all; it carries its own benefits which are enshrined in the blessing, and yet some still refuse it. Living a kingdom life requires you to accept the King into your life and make Him the centre. Once the King takes up throne in your heart, light begins to shine in your path as long as He stays inside. And how do I keep Him inside? By following His statutes and harkening to His commands (the Word) as the King, for the King and His Word are one and inseparable. As for me, I have seen the light and I will follow it because it leads to eternal life.

Choose this day what team you want to be on. The Bible says be either hot or cold. You cannot be both (Revelation 3:15–16). You cannot have one leg in team Spiritual and another in team Worldly. Choose which team to stick with because you cannot be lukewarm; otherwise God will spew you out. The reason why sometimes Christianity doesn't seem to work for some is because we have taken the pure things of God and mixed them with the profane. You cannot mix idle worship and godliness; you cannot mix godliness and worldliness (evil works, corruption and crookedness, the world's way of doing things which is contrary to God's ways). We are in this world but not of this world. We have defiled the purity of godliness (character and principles) by mixing it with strange wine. Therefore such an equation will not produce results.

When you have Jesus Christ in you, you have the resurrection power at work in you. Visions, dreams, and every good thing that had died have to resurrect, because the hope of glory dwells inside of you. That's the power in that wonderful name. John 3:16; "For God so loved the world that He gave His only begotten son, that whosoever believes in Him will not perish, but have everlasting life!" Amen! Let the giver of life be at the centre of your heart, and nothing about you concerning life shall perish!

Whatever hinders your walk with Christ, lay it aside. Be it anger, unforgiveness, hatred, bitterness, worldliness, unfaithfulness, lay it aside and enjoy the benefits and also the trials that come with following Jesus, knowing that you have a far much greater eternal reward. Lay aside every feeling of hurt, regret, shame, and guilt as well. It cripples your faith in Him who is merciful, just, and full of love and grace. His name is Love, and He desires to forgive you of all the darkest and dirtiest things you might have done, and love you with all that He's got. One thing I love about God is that when He forgives you, He makes it as if you never even committed the sin in the first place. Our transgression is blotted out and never to be remembered again. Woe unto him who dares unravel what the Lord has done away with and forgiven. Run to His wide open arms and receive rest in Him. You are loved beyond human comprehension!

Purpose in your heart to make Jesus Christ the centre of your very being!

The Conclusion of the Matter

Live and lead a purpose-driven life and enjoy it. Life is meant to be enjoyable; have a blast! But know that with every action there will always be consequences, so make sure you gravitate in the right direction. Learn to make wise decisions or choices. Have an amazing positive attitude. Follow that voice deep inside of you called instinct, or the Holy Spirit. Be bold, be courageous, spread your wings like an eagle, and fly. Be adventurous, and explore different options; make the journey dynamic, and add colour to it. In whatever you might want to achieve, never allow yourself to be stuck in a box. It could be the "box" of skin colour, gender, nationality, or a physical disability that might have crippled you; but I'm here to let you know that as long as you have the power of the mind, as long as your brain still functions, as long as you have the willpower to dream, you can still be unstoppable, because the barriers we create are only in our minds! As long as you can overcome the barriers in your mind, you can do absolutely anything! Whatever your mind can conceive, you can achieve it. Never allow other people's ill feelings and thoughts towards you to bring you down; don't give away your personal power like that.

Let integrity and good morals be your guide. Remember, moderation is key. Do everything in moderation. Make the journey interesting. Don't be stuck in unproductive cycles and circles. Be bold in your choices, stand your ground, break the rules (anything that limits you), and create your own rules. Be innovative, creative, industrious, and always optimistic. Never allow fear to cripple you, either. What is it that you are afraid of? Whatever it is, it can be overcome as long as you put your mind to it. Stop making excuses; you are an achiever. You were designed to contribute something significant in this life. Aim to leave a legacy. Live a lifestyle of prayer. Always put Jesus Christ at the centre of it all, because when He is in the centre, just like the nucleus of an atom, everything else is kept in place; nothing falls apart.

Live your dream, sing your song, do your dance, spread your wings and fly. Live life in abundance and enjoy the ride! Don't forget to write down your principles and stick them somewhere visible as a reminder. Be principled and consistent in application of your principles.

Love,
David Conellias

Slow down and enjoy Life. Life happens so quickly. Things change so rapidly. It's important that we live our Lives to the maximum. Don't let Life pass you by. Laugh a lot! Hug a lot! And Smile for no reason. There's always a reason to be thankful.

-Lewis Hamilton

I Choose

I choose to live by choice, and not by chance.
I choose to make changes, and not excuses.
I choose to be motivated, and not manipulated.
I choose to be useful, and not to be taken advantage of.
I choose to excel, and not to compete *(trying to compete with
someone can lead to jealousy, strife, debate, having a deceitful
spirit, greed, envy, and being malicious and slanderous)*.
I choose self-esteem, and not self-pity.
I choose to listen to the inner voice, and not
the random opinion of others.
I choose to have a positive mentality, and
denounce a negative attitude.
I choose to keep moving forward, and not
to dwell on my past failures.
I choose to be joyful, and never to drown in sorrows.
I choose to love and forgive, and never to hold a grudge.
I choose to be a peacemaker, and not a warlord.
I choose to respect others, and mind my own business.
I choose to be courteous, and not rude or arrogant.
I choose to be generous, and not self-centred.
I choose to give, and never withhold from those in need.
I choose to make wise decisions and choices,
and never to be irrational or naive.
I choose to live life with purpose and direction,
and not just wander and drift aimlessly.
I choose to educate myself, and never to sit on my brain.
As a man thinketh, so is he; therefore I choose to
steer my thoughts in a positive direction.
I choose to become all that I was designed
to be, and to live authentically.
I choose to lead in all areas of life.

I choose to stand for what is right, upholding good ethical
morals, and never backing down from my stance or beliefs.
I choose to celebrate people's differences, with the
knowledge that each person is unique.
I choose to be humble, knowing that I will be lifted up.
It's better to be humble than to be humiliated.
I choose to leave a good legacy for generations to follow, and
a good name which is better than precious ointment.
I choose to be principled, maintaining strong character and
integrity. I will not be influenced by peer pressure!
I choose the reverential fear of the Lord, which
is the beginning of all wisdom.
I choose to be bold and courageous, and never to be a slave to fear.
I choose to have eyes that see the best, and
a heart that forgives the worst.
I choose to enjoy and live life, and not to worry about life!

The 59 "One Anothers" of the New Testament

1. "Be at peace with each other." (Mark 9:50)
2. "Wash one another's feet." (John 13:14)
3. "Love one another." (John 13:34a)
4. "Love one another." (John 13:34b)
5. "Love one another." (John 13:35)
6. "Love one another." (John 15:12)
7. "Love one another." (John 15:17)
8. "Be devoted to one another in brotherly love." (Romans 12:10)
9. "Honour one another above yourselves." (Romans 12:10)
10. "Live in harmony with one another." (Romans 12:16)
11. "Love one another." (Romans 13:8)
12. "Stop passing judgment on one another." (Romans 14:13)
13. "Accept one another, then, just as Christ accepted you." (Romans 15:7)
14. "Instruct one another." (Romans 15:14)
15. "Greet one another with a holy kiss." (Romans 16:16)
16. "When you come together to eat, wait for each other." (I Cor. 11:33)
17. "Have equal concern for each other." (I Corinthians 12:25)
18. "Greet one another with a holy kiss." (I Corinthians 16:20)
19. "Greet one another with a holy kiss." (II Corinthians 13:12)
20. "Serve one another in love." (Galatians 5:13)
21. "If you keep on biting and devouring each other … you will be destroyed by each other." (Galatians 5:15)

22. "Let us not become conceited, provoking and envying each other." (Galatians 5:26)
23. "Carry each other's burdens." (Galatians 6:2)
24. "Be patient, bearing with one another in love." (Ephesians 4:2)
25. "Be kind and compassionate to one another." (Ephesians 4:32)
26. "Forgiving each other." (Ephesians 4:32)
27. "Speak to one another with psalms, hymns and spiritual songs." (Ephesians 5:19)
28. "Submit to one another out of reverence for Christ." (Ephesians 5:21)
29. "In humility consider others better than yourselves." (Philippians 2:3)
30. "Do not lie to each other." (Colossians 3:9)
31. "Bear with each other." (Colossians 3:13)
32. "Forgive whatever grievances you may have against one another." (Colossians 3:13)
33. "Teach … [one another]." (Colossians 3:16)
34. "Admonish one another." (Colossians 3:16)
35. "Make your love increase and overflow for each other." (I Thessalonians 3:12)
36. "Love each other." (I Thessalonians 4:9)
37. "Encourage each other."(I Thessalonians 4:18)
38. "Encourage each other." I Thessalonians 5:11)
39. "Build each other up." (I Thessalonians 5:11)
40. "Encourage one another daily." (Hebrews 3:13)
41. "Spur one another on toward love and good deeds." (Hebrews 10:24)
42. "Encourage one another." (Hebrews 10:25)
43. "Do not slander one another." (James 4:11)
44. "Don't grumble against each other." (James 5:9)
45. "Confess your sins to each other." (James 5:16)
46. "Pray for each other." (James 5:16)
47. "Love one another deeply, from the heart." (I Peter 3:8)
48. "Live in harmony with one another." (I Peter 3:8)
49. "Love each other deeply." (I Peter 4:8)

50. "Offer hospitality to one another without grumbling."
    (I Peter 4:9)
51. "Each one should use whatever gift he has received to serve others." (I Peter 4:10)
52. "Clothe yourselves with humility toward one another."
    (I Peter 5:5)
53. "Greet one another with a kiss of love."
    (simply means affectionately) (I Peter 5:14)
54. "Love one another." (I John 3:11)
55. "Love one another." (I John 3:23)
56. "Love one another." (I John 4:7)
57. "Love one another." (I John 4:11)
58. "Love one another." (I John 4:12)
59. "Love one another." (II John 5)
    -Andrew Mason

PERSONAL EMPOWERMENT QUOTES/NOTES

➤ Hang around the best, and become the best. Good company contains and improves good morals, and bad company corrupts good morals.

➤ The Word of God is the perfect Life Manual. Read it and extract inspiration and power from it.

➤ Steer clear of peer pressure. Just because everybody else is doing it doesn't make it right. Be your own person; choose to stand out and make the right choices.

➤ I was never created to fit it; I was created to stand out. Eagles do not flock, let alone with chickens! Dare to stand out.

➤ Do not let money be your god, but let God be your money. When you have God, you have access to what money can't buy. When you have God, you have a reliable and sure means of exchange. Jehovah Jireh.

➤ Determination will lead you to your destination.

➤ Life should be vibrant and dynamic. Accept change, and even *make* some changes along the way.

➤ Future blessing depends on present obedience.

➤ You are who you think you are, and you are what you say you are.

➤ God gave *everyone* the gift of the mind. Use that power to control your thoughts to whatever ends you desire.

➤ True love makes no excuses; it makes an effort.

➤ Love like you will never get the chance again! Don't be afraid to express this beautiful emotion. True love has no barriers or limits; it cuts through the toughest of walls and heals the soul!

➤ An abandoned pond attracts all sorts of dirt and insects (disease and illnesses). Stir up your waters and exercise for healthy living.

➤ It's not how and where you start that matters; it's how you finish. Better is the end of a thing than its beginning.

➤ It is a miserable lion that wishes to be a giraffe. Be authentic, be who God made you to be, and stop desiring to be someone else.

➤ Ignorance is your worst enemy. What you don't know might be killing you.

➤ Watch your words, watch your thoughts. Harness them and direct them to whatsoever ends you desire to see in life.

➤ Harboured hatred is like acid that eats your soul and body away! Release that acid by forgiving.

➤ In life, you attract what you celebrate and repel what you don't. When you see others succeed and you celebrate them, that success will also follow you. But if you are jealous, you repel the success! Same for everything else.

➤ Moderation is key; too much of something is not good.

➤ A little positive thought in the morning can set the right mood for the rest of the day. The same goes for a little negative thought.

➤ Be faithful with the little first, and you'll be made a steward of bigger and greater things.

➤ Have forward vision; your eyes are in front for a reason! *(Remember ye not the former things, neither consider the things of old.)*

➤ Every answer I'm looking for is inside of me. All I need to do is to dig deeper and extract what God has put inside of me. God has encoded everything I would ever need in life into my DNA. I don't have to look far because I have the answer already. Follow your instinct.

➤ Being stingy only leads to more poverty, but the generous hand is made rich.

➤ Successful people are not quitters; quitting is never an option for them. If you want to go far in life, never quit, despite the opposition and challenges along the road.

➢ Generous people are the happiest people alive.

➢ Success or failure in business is caused more by the mental attitude, than by mental capacities.

➢ Before a person can achieve the kind of life he wants, he must think, act, walk, talk, and conduct his affairs as would the person he wishes to become.

➢ Prayer and Praise are our weapons of mass destruction.

➢ Patience is a virtue, don't be rush to make decisions without proper judgement.

➢ Actions speak louder than words. Be wary of the contradiction between your words and your actions. Let both match up!

Quotes by Other People

❖ Well done is better than well said. —Benjamin Franklin

❖ Your attitude is an outward expression of an inward feeling. —John C. Maxwell

❖ Two things to remember in life: Take care of your thoughts when you are alone, and take care of your words when you are with people.

❖ Run when you can, walk if you have to, crawl if you must; but just never give up.

❖ Put God first, and you will never be last!

❖ To be the best, you must be able to handle the worst.

❖ Strong people don't put others down, they lift them up. —Michael P. Watson

❖ Don't find fault, find a remedy. —Henry Ford

❖ The situation you live doesn't have to live in you. —Roberta Flack

❖ Attitude is the criterion for success. But you can't buy an attitude for a million dollars. Attitudes are not for sale. —Denis Waitley

❖ Man who say it cannot be done should not interrupt man doing it. —Chinese Proverb

❖ When you affirm big, believe big, and pray big, big things happen. —Norman Vincent Peale

- If you have a will to win, you have achieved half your success; if you don't, you have achieved half your failure. —David Ambrose
- You can get everything in life you want, if you help enough other people get what they want. —Zig Ziglar
- Always help people increase their own self-esteem. Develop your skill in making other people feel important. —Donald Laird
- Always make others feel needed, important, and appreciated and they'll return the same to you. —John C. Maxwell
- The greatest mistake one can make in life is to be continually fearing you will make one. —Elbert Hubbard
- Worry does not help anything, but it hurts everything. —George S. Patton
- Anybody who accepts mediocrity in school, on the job, in life, is a person who compromises, and when the leader compromises, the whole organisation compromises. —Charles Knight
- Nothing can stop the man with right mental attitude from achieving his goal; nothing on earth can help the man with wrong mental attitude. —W.W. Ziege
- A successful man is one who can lay a firm foundation with the bricks others have thrown at him. —David Brinkley
- Attitude is contagious, is yours worth catching? —Dr. Walter Masocha
- Health, happiness, and prosperity are primarily mental. —Marian Ramsay
- Man's greatness lies in his power of thought. —Blaise Pascal
- The quality of a person's life is in direct proportion to their commitment to excellence, regardless of their chosen field of endeavour. —Vince Lombardi
- Anyone who stops learning is old, whether at twenty or eighty. Anyone who keeps learning stays young. —Henry Ford
- It is no exaggeration to say that a strong, positive self-image is the best possible preparation for success in life. —Dr. Joyce Brothers

- Most folks are as happy as they make up their minds to be. —Abraham Lincoln

- Better to remain silent and be thought a fool, than to speak out and remove all doubt. —Abraham Lincoln

- Sir, my concern is not whether God is on our side; my greatest concern is to be on God's side, for God is always right. —Abraham Lincoln

- Life is too short to spend your precious time trying to convince a person who wants to live in gloom and doom otherwise. Give lifting that person your best shot, but don't hang around long enough for his or her bad attitude to pull you down. Instead surround yourself with positive people. —Zig Ziglar

- Character is like a tree and reputation like a shadow. The shadow is what we think of it; the tree is the real thing. —Abraham Lincoln

- In the end, it's not the years in your life that count. It's the life in your years. —Abraham Lincoln

- A friend is the one who has the same enemies as you have. —Abraham Lincoln

- You have to do your own growing no matter how tall your grandfather was. —Abraham Lincoln

- Logic will get you from A to B. Imagination will take you everywhere. —Albert Einstein

- Successful people are always looking for opportunities to help others. Unsuccessful people are always asking; "what's in it for me?" —Brian Tracey

I am David Conellias, The Man after God's Own Heart, Possessor of The Blessing, Highly Favoured and Esteemed, The Apple of God's Eye, An Eagle in Motion, A Trailblazer and Trendsetter, A Powerful Force of Nature, A Citizen Of The Kingdom Of Heaven, and I Positively Impact the Trajectory of Humanity!

Amen!

Periodic Table of The Elements

This table might not make sense to some people, but it's only there for illustration purposes, in support of Principle #20.